To Emmanuelle,

I hope that you will
feel even closer to your
family and to God as you're
this. Please email me + let
me know what you think!

love,
Kristen

Heritage Restored

THE DEMPS, BOOKER, AND ESTELL FAMILIES

KRISTEN A. ANDERSEN

Heritage Restored: The Demps, Booker and Estelle Families Copyright © 2010 Kristen Amille Andersen

ISBN: 1-453-66966-3

FIRST EDITION

Printed in the United States of America

Photos on cover and front page are courtesy of Margaret Willis, Charlenia Curry, and U.V. Estelle, Jr.
Front cover, Left to right, top row: Larry Demps boxing; Gary Demps on horse; Nellie Demps with her first four children. *Bottom row*: Charles and Nellie Demps at their daughter Margaret's wedding; Richard Booker, U.V. Estelle, Jr., Richard, Joe, and Joseph Booker
Title page, on top row: Charles Demps, Jr., Christine Demps, Charlenia Demps, and Margaret Demps at school in Sylacauga.
Photos on back cover: "Cotton Picking Time at Avondale Mills," from *The Avondale Sun*; U.V. Estelle with his car; Demps family gathering, Kristen Andersen at Estell Lane.

To Grandma

Soft and warm
like a thick quilt pieced together
slowly, deliberately,
hand-stitched with patience

Your love enveloped me

Rested comfortably upon my soul
like a blanket tucked tenderly around
tiny hands and feet

Gently untangled my heartaches
like work-worn fingers combing through
long tangled tresses

Softly sang truth to my spirit
an instrument of healing and protection

You had my whole world in your hands.

- Kristen Andersen -

TABLE OF CONTENTS

ACKNOWLEDGEMENTS

*F*AMILY history research cannot be done alone. I am so grateful to the many friends and family members who have helped me to make this dream become a reality.

First, I would like to thank those who took time to help me piece together the history of our family. Margaret Willis, Charlenia Curry, Doris Banks, U.V. Jr. and Patricia Estelle, Lavonne Morris, Lena Gudiel-Teo, Booker T. Booker, Jr., Louise White, Patricia Lyles, Rita Morrison, and Mary J. Peterson not only helped me with stories, documents, and pictures, but each of them took an interest in this project and supported me from the moment we first talked about it. They have truly been family to me, and that means more to me than they know.

Special thanks to Glenn Drummond at the Macon County Archives, Frazine Taylor at the Alabama Department of Archives and History, the Tuskegee and the Sylacauga Public Libraries, and the staff at the Macon County and Talladega County Probate Offices. They were helpful and patient as we scoured records from opening to closing time. Thanks also to my fellow consultants and friends at the Coral Springs LDS Family History Center as well, for making microfilm research so much fun!

My deepest gratitude goes to Dr. Kathleen Ward for encouraging me long ago to take on a project like this, as well as my dear friends Karin Bowman and Janalie Joseph, who helped with page layout, editing, and ideas in moments of writer's block. I am thankful for their time, effort, and friendship.

This would not have been possible without the unfailing support of my sweet husband, Jon. He became my research assistant on excursions through Michigan and Alabama, patiently waited up at night when I was on the brink of a fascinating discovery, and cried or rejoiced with me depending on what information came on the records in the mail. He is my companion and friend, and I am grateful to be building eternal family relationships with him.

Most of all, I am thankful to my Father in heaven for directing me as I have done this research. This has been hard work, and I have felt the hand of the Lord in every step. I believe the words of the prophet Malachi in the Bible, who said, "And he shall turn the heart of the fathers to the children, and the heart of the children to their fa-thers" (Malachi 4:6). I believe that we are all God's children. This research has given me a greater appreciation for our ancestors, for the lives they lived, and for the sacrifices that they made. I am so grateful for the blessings of God that have given me the opportunity to not only do this research, but to put together a history for others to read, therefore sharing these blessings with my family and friends. I have come to know myself more through knowing our ancestors, and that has been a heavenly gift to me.

INTRODUCTION

*I*N West Africa, each family or village had a *griot*: the storyteller who kept the traditions and history, and made sure that they were passed from one generation to the next. Out of all of my first cousins, I am the youngest, so perhaps this is why I have felt so compelled to preserve the family history.

My interest started in seventh grade when I had to do a family tree project for school. The tree was enormous! It took three full poster boards to lay out the whole tree, and it wasn't even comprehensive; it was just my grandparents' siblings, their parents, my aunts, uncles, and cousins.

There were names that always stuck out to me: Es Estell, Joe Booker, Henry Demps, and Annie

Senegalese Griot, ca. 1890

Magruder. I felt like I wanted to know them, even though they lived so long ago. I had done some research here and there over the years, but it wasn't until my grandmother, Nellie Booker Demps, passed away that I felt the urgency to commit our family history to paper. After her passing, I learned that she and I had in common this passion to preserve our family history; sadly, I never truly realized it while she was alive. I found out how many pictures she really had, how she had saved everything, and how she (and later Auntie Marie) had been paying taxes for several decades on land owned by her grandfather, Sherman Booker, to keep it in the family. The history of the family was important to her, and I could feel a connection to our history running through me as I started preserving her photos and as I set foot on that family land, owned by our forefathers who were born just before slavery ended.

A few years ago, my Auntie Marie showed me some of my grandmother's quilts that she was restoring. They were beautiful! I never even knew they existed until she brought them out. Being somewhat familiar with the time and labor that goes into the process of quilting, I was impressed that my grandmother could make such beautiful quilts while fulfilling her other responsibilities as a wife, mother, and head of household while her husband worked nearly eight hundred miles away from the family. I was equally impressed with Auntie Marie's undertaking to restore the quilts. She had to search through the whole quilt for places where the stitches were weak or missing and carefully reinforce them with thread,

Skeletons in the Closet

When I was young, my dad had a beebee gun hidden in the back of his bedroom closet. Just so that I wouldn't play with it, he told me that there were skeletons in the closet and that I shouldn't go in there. Because I was young, I was very scared and decided that there must be skeletons in *all* the closets! As much as he meant to protect me from getting hurt, perhaps teaching me the truth about dangerous objects would have worked better. I didn't touch the stove after he taught me it was hot.

Often I think the same goes for family history. People hide secrets, or "skeletons in the closet," about family members, usually out of the innocent intention of protecting others from the pain that the truthful information might cause. Instead, people end up confused, mistrustful, or even more hurt when they find out the truth later on. It seems better to deal with touchy issues as they are, even if they are difficult or sensitive.

These sections will be devoted to bringing out some of those tougher issues, the "skeletons in the closet." I believe that knowing the truth about family secrets or painting a full picture of someone's life gives us a greater context for our own lives. We can see why people are the way they are, how certain patterns may have been established, and most importantly, that we don't have to repeat negative patterns in our own lives and families.

following the old stitches. This process made the quilt spring back to life and preserved it for many more generations to enjoy.

Likewise, my research journey has been one of combing through records, filling in the missing links, and sometimes bringing out stories that no one knew existed. It has been a process of restoring our lost history so that our ancestors' stories can spring back to life and be enjoyed by all of us for many more decades.

This history comes mostly from a combination

One of Nellie Booker Demps' handmade quilts.

of several types of government and family records, as well as from stories and information gathered from various members of the family. I have done my best to piece it all together into a clear picture of how our

ancestors lived, so this history will include both the positive and negative aspects that comprise the story of their lives. There are a few individuals for which there was very little or no information available. In those cases, I have made it clear that I had to speculate about them based on historical events or other information available during that time period. It is also a history from my own perspective, and while I have tried to make it both historically accurate and informative, I have also included some of my own experiences and feelings. Preserving the history of our ancestors has connected me to my grandparents and the ancestors before them.

My hope is that you will feel that same connec-

Photo: Kristen Andersen Collection

tion running through you as you read these stories and see the actual documents that have been preserved since the 1800s, bearing the names and life events of our ancestors. I hope that you will learn lessons from their stories that will help you to live better lives today and tomorrow. Our ancestors and our history deserve to be recorded and remembered. As we go forward, learning from their experiences, we can take positive action, having hope for the future and pride in ourselves and in how far we have come as a family and as individuals. Our ancestors will be proud of us for this. ✾

DEMPS, BOOKER AND ESTELL FAMILY TREE

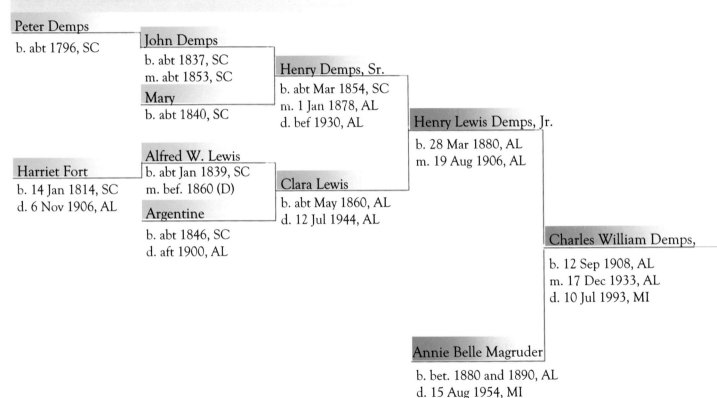

Peter Demps
b. abt 1796, SC

John Demps
b. abt 1837, SC
m. abt 1853, SC

Mary
b. abt 1840, SC

Henry Demps, Sr.
b. abt Mar 1854, SC
m. 1 Jan 1878, AL
d. bef 1930, AL

Henry Lewis Demps, Jr.
b. 28 Mar 1880, AL
m. 19 Aug 1906, AL

Harriet Fort
b. 14 Jan 1814, SC
d. 6 Nov 1906, AL

Alfred W. Lewis
b. abt Jan 1839, SC
m. bef. 1860 (D)

Argentine
b. abt 1846, SC
d. aft 1900, AL

Clara Lewis
b. abt May 1860, AL
d. 12 Jul 1944, AL

Charles William Demps,
b. 12 Sep 1908, AL
m. 17 Dec 1933, AL
d. 10 Jul 1993, MI

Annie Belle Magruder
b. bet. 1880 and 1890, AL
d. 15 Aug 1954, MI

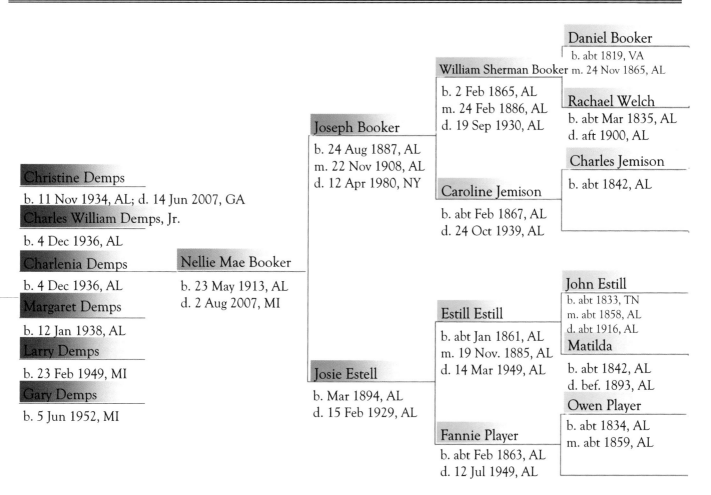

Christine Demps
b. 11 Nov 1934, AL; d. 14 Jun 2007, GA
Charles William Demps, Jr.
b. 4 Dec 1936, AL
Charlenia Demps
b. 4 Dec 1936, AL
Margaret Demps
b. 12 Jan 1938, AL
Larry Demps
b. 23 Feb 1949, MI
Gary Demps
b. 5 Jun 1952, MI

Nellie Mae Booker
b. 23 May 1913, AL
d. 2 Aug 2007, MI

Joseph Booker
b. 24 Aug 1887, AL
m. 22 Nov 1908, AL
d. 12 Apr 1980, NY

Josie Estell
b. Mar 1894, AL
d. 15 Feb 1929, AL

William Sherman Booker
b. 2 Feb 1865, AL
m. 24 Feb 1886, AL
d. 19 Sep 1930, AL

Caroline Jemison
b. abt Feb 1867, AL
d. 24 Oct 1939, AL

Estill Estill
b. abt Jan 1861, AL
m. 19 Nov. 1885, AL
d. 14 Mar 1949, AL

Fannie Player
b. abt Feb 1863, AL
d. 12 Jul 1949, AL

Daniel Booker
b. abt 1819, VA
m. 24 Nov 1865, AL

Rachael Welch
b. abt Mar 1835, AL
d. aft 1900, AL

Charles Jemison
b. abt 1842, AL

John Estill
b. abt 1833, TN
m. abt 1858, AL
d. abt 1916, AL

Matilda
b. abt 1842, AL
d. bef. 1893, AL

Owen Player
b. abt 1834, AL
m. abt 1859, AL

SECTION ONE:

CHARLES WILLIAM DEMPS, SR.

Nothing ever comes to one, that is worth having, except as a result of hard work.
– Booker T. Washington –

Charles William Demps

CHARLES William Demps, Sr. wore out his life working. Before 1930, when Charles was still only a teenager, his father had abandoned the family. At the young age of 19, Charles was called upon to help support his brothers and sister, as well as his mother. Because his older brother, John Henry, had a heart condition and was often sick, Charles became the head of the household. Surely this was a heavy burden for him, yet he took that responsibility seriously and continued to look after his siblings and mother throughout his life, even after establishing his own family. Charles, David, and Annie worked as farm laborers, and John Henry used his skills as a shoe repairman to bring in income. Together they supported one another and their mother through difficult times.

In 1933, their family began to change. October brought the marriage of Charles' sister, Annie, to a man named Doyle Young (whom she quickly divorced). Only two months later, on December 17th, Charles married Nellie Mae Booker at her home in Sycamore. They started a family right away, so in November 1934 their first child, Christine, was born. The nation was still recovering from the Great Depression, fighting to survive through unemployment, drought, food shortages, extreme poverty, and general hopelessness. Yet in

Margaret Willis Collection

1935, while most people in the country were putting their lives back together or worrying about their next meal, Charles was able to buy a plot of land on which he and Nellie built their first home and raised four children.

Over the years Charles was able to find better employment and provide for his growing family. He found work quarrying marble in Sylacauga, Alabama, most likely at the famous Gantts Quarry. Marble extracted from this quarry was used in creating the Washington Monument and the Lincoln Memorial, and is some of the finest marble in the world.[1] The work was hard, and many men suffered severe health problems as a result of the working conditions.

A Complex Individual

I only knew Grandpa one way: hugs and baseball, checkers and Freedent gum. But painting a portrait of his life in this way would really only cover his last 15 years. Charles was also a drinker, and he loved his cigars (as you can see in even his earliest photos). He smiled very little in pictures before 1980; in fact, he looked flat out mean and disinterested in most of them. Several people have told stories about how angry he would get, and many grandchildren remember the beatings they received from him for little or no reason. His own children likely suffered even more. Charles was also known to sometimes talk with other women when attending music shows, whether or not his wife was present. Even Nellie, in the late stages of her Alzheimer's disease, loosed her tongue and had some pretty angry (albeit honest) words to say about her late husband, his drinking, and his treatment of her as an object.

Patterns like this are usually picked up somewhere: in Charles' case, probably from his father who left while Charles was only a teenager. They are also usually passed down as well, since this is the behavior that the children witness in their home every day. Some of the results have been alcohol and drug problems, anger issues, and struggling marriages over the years, sometimes hidden from the rest of the family. Fortunately, at some point Charles quit smoking and drinking, and he did not treat his younger grandchildren and great-grandchildren with the same harshness. I do not know what caused this change, but it does not excuse his previous behavior, nor does it take away the effects of his actions on his family. We must each choose to deal with that ourselves, and to protect our children by not repeating the same behaviors in our own families.

One of the Alabama Marble Company Quarries at Gantts Quarry, Alabama.

Margaret Willis Collection

Charles and Nellie's first home in Sylacauga, Alabama

tions throughout Alabama, including Sycamore, Pell City, and Birmingham. These textile mills did everything from growing and picking cotton to spinning it into thread, to then weaving it into fabric and dying it so it could be sold and made into clothing. Working in a textile mill was very tedious work, but it paid better than farming and was definitely safer than working at the quarry. And even with a young family and his mother to provide for, somehow Charles was making enough to save on the side.

Quarrying often required shoveling heavy loads of broken rocks, or moving cut stones by hand, causing serious back and spinal injuries. In addition, the dust caused by cutting the stones often led to chronic lung diseases.

Fortunately, Charles did not have to work at the quarry for long. He soon found employment at Avondale Mills in Sylacauga, a textile manufacturing facility. They were one of the most prosperous textile mills in the country, with facilities in several loca-

Photo courtesy www.Gutenberg.org

Cotton mill workers in the fields ca. 1920

Eventually, Charles saved enough to make several more land purchases. On a few occasions Charles and his brother, David, pooled their resources and bought land together. Charles' main focus, though, was to provide for his family. With his wife Nellie, Charles purchased land in a section of Sylacauga called Oakland Heights, so that their children would have land in case they ever needed somewhere to live. Some of that land is still in the family today.

The United States became involved in World War II in 1941, and although Charles' age disqualified him from fighting as a soldier, he did contribute to the war effort. In February of 1942, he began working for the Alabama Ordnance Works, located in Childersburg, Alabama. The plant produced powder munitions and dangerous chemicals to be used in the atomic bomb.[2]

Soon the time came for Charles to make an important decision that was on the minds of many African-Americans after the war: whether to stay in the

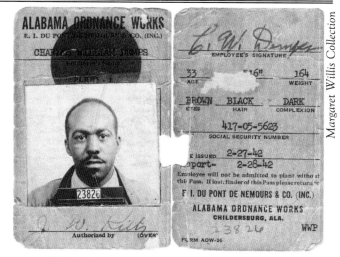

Margaret Willis Collection

Work identification card for employment at the Alabama Ordnance Works

South or to seek new opportunities for employment and happiness in the North. Charles chose the latter, and in doing so became part of the Great Migration. In 1946 Charles left his family temporarily to seek employment. He moved to Detroit, Michigan, and there he found a job on the assembly lines at the Chrysler Corporation. In 1948, he and Nellie sold off their land, and by July the entire family had

Photo courtesy of Windsor Star

Chrysler assembly line in 1957.

moved to Detroit, to a home on Fleming Street. Assembly line work was stressful, not always because of the difficulty of the work, but because of the repetitive nature of the labor. As a welder, Charles likely welded the same piece of metal in the same location on up to 100 cars an hour. The repetition caused injuries in some people, and many people coped with the everyday monotony through addictions.[3] But the job paid well enough that Charles could be a consistent provider for his family. His steady employment made it possible for Nellie to be a full-time homemaker and to take care of their family of six children. It also provided the means for him to take care of his mother until she died in their home in Detroit. He provided space for extended family when they were down on their luck, even when it meant cramped living quarters for a while. Working for Chrysler also gave Charles a love for cars that never ceased and that was unmatched by anyone I have ever known. He worked for Chrysler until his retirement.

Charles William Demps, Sr. was my grandpa, and I loved him. I remember being five or six years old, driving down I-696 from Milford to

Margaret Willis Collection

Charles around 1988

Jacksonville Historical Society

Charles played for a Negro baseball team at work much like this one.

Detroit, excitedly anticipating our arrival at Grandma and Grandpa's house on Asbury Park. Grandpa smelled like Freedent gum, and when he asked me to "give him some sugar," my face was always shocked by the scratchy gray stubble on his cheek as I gave him a great big kiss.

We would play checkers on the front porch for a while and then Grandpa would go inside and watch a game of baseball on the television. Sometimes I would creep into the back room and just stare at the old black and white picture of him in his baseball uniform from his days of playing on his Avondale Mills company team, AVONDALE written boldly across the front. Whenever I saw that photo, I felt proud of him for playing the game he loved so much.

Even though Grandpa had faults and made many mistakes in his life, there are still lessons I have learned from the good that he did. I have learned that we really can change our circumstances if we work hard enough, even if it means making some short-term sacrifices. The work that we do to change our circumstances may change the lives of several generations after us. From Grandpa I have also learned to take care of things that are gifts or that we work hard to receive. He always treated his car like it was a gift, and kept it looking brand new. Perhaps that was his way of trying to look good to the neighbors, but for me, it was a way of making things last that you have worked for, and expressing gratitude to God for the gifts that He gives us by taking good care of them.✵

HENRY LEWIS DEMPS, JR. & ANNIE BELLE MAGRUDER

*Suffering breeds character, character breeds faith.
In the end faith will not disappoint.*
— Jesse Jackson—

Photo courtesy Auburn University Library Special Collections

$\mathscr{G}$ROWING up in the rural areas of western Macon County, Alabama in the 1880s was understandably difficult. Families were adjusting to a life of freedom from slavery while still doing very much the same work alongside the same people. In many cases, African-Americans still depended on white families for rented land and basic security. Each day was a struggle for each family to survive while trying to come out ahead financially—or at least break even. Henry Lewis Demps, Jr. was born into these circumstances.

Henry was the eldest of five boys. Born in Cross Keys, Alabama in 1880, he went unnamed for at least two months.

Annie likely worked hard in the fields every day as a farm laborer, much like this woman plowing with her ox.

Finally, his parents named him after his father, choosing his mother's maiden name, Lewis, for his middle name. By 1900 the Demps family moved to La Place, and Henry had already started working for others as a farm laborer in the community. This meant that he tended someone else's farm for daily wages, in addition to helping out with his own family's farm work and chores. Daily farm labor became terribly monotonous though, so once a month on a Saturday, wagons full of young men and women would take the journey into Tuskegee to relax and enjoy themselves, leaving behind the stresses of everyday life. Perhaps it was on one of these trips that Henry met a young woman from Tuskegee named Annie Belle Magruder, who later became his wife.

Unfortunately, no one knows very much about Annie, who was born sometime between 1880 and 1890 near Tuskegee, Alabama. (The 1890 census was completely destroyed in a fire, so information from this time period is largely unavailable.) The name 'Annie Belle Magruder' was very popular, though: there were at least three other girls given this name who were born in the same area during the same time period. Searching for this particular Annie is therefore much more difficult. Annie likely grew up in a family who were employed as farm laborers, as that was the most common work among black men and women in Macon county at that time. By the time she was an adult, Annie was probably employed as a farm laborer herself. It was during this time that she met and fell in love with Henry. On August 19, 1906, they were married in La Place, Alabama and moved to a small farm there. Henry and Annie both worked as farm laborers after their marriage. The common arrangement in this situation was for both husband and wife to work on someone else's farm for daily wages (about 40 to 50 cents per day), with a little patch of ground of their own to cultivate, and a run-down cabin to live in rent-free.

Within a year, Henry and Annie welcomed their first son, John Henry Demps, in March of 1907. Henry and Annie were married seven months when John Henry was born, and he was likely born early. He suffered throughout his life with the consequences of a congenital heart defect (a problem with his heart that was present when he was born). Such heart defects can be passed on genetically, or they can be the result of a mother contracting the Rubella virus during pregnancy. There were no treatments or medications for heart defects, so his parents did the best they could to take care of him and help him grow.

The next year, Charles William (nicknamed

'Charlie Will') was born in September 1908, and in January 1910, David Lee joined their family. By this time, Annie Belle was cooking meals, doing laundry, taking care of two young, energetic boys and a newborn, laboring on the farm of a white family, and trying to help grow some crops to feed her own family. This was not the ideal situation for a young mother. She must have been tired, but she endured in her work to support her family.

Life continued this way for most people in rural Macon County; people farmed and raised their families, and every so often moved from one tenant farm in the county to another, but they almost never left the county where they were born. Something different was in store for Henry, Annie, and their family, though.

In June 1912, Henry and Annie had their last child, a daughter named Annie Pearl Clara Demps. A few years later, Henry found an opportunity to work for better pay on the construction of a new rail-

1910 US Census listing Henry and Annie and their occupations in Anniston, AL (Courtesy of Ancestry.com)

road through Alabama. Around 1915, the entire family moved to Anniston, Alabama, about 125 miles north of Tuskegee in Calhoun County. They rented a small apartment on Cooper Avenue in the housing built for the Louisville and Nashville Railroad workers which was only about 750 feet from the railroad.

Henry worked on the L&N Railroad as part of a section gang, which is a crew assigned to maintain a specific portion of the railroad: replacing rotted wooden ties, clearing weeds, and most importantly, keeping the rails straight. Each time a train barreled down the tracks, the force of the train would move the tracks slightly out of place. Workers were needed to put the tracks back into place regularly so that the trains would not derail. These railroad workers were sometimes known as "gandy dancers."[1] The workers used calls, or special songs, to help along the grueling work of shoving the railroad tracks back into place. Each of them held a tool called a gandy to push

World War I Draft Registration card of Henry Lewis Demps. (Courtesy of Ancestry.com)

the track, and the rhythm of the call helped them to coordinate their efforts, throw their weight, and push all at the same time. Perhaps the movement to the rhythm of the call invoked the name "dancer" upon these particular railroad workers. The work was exhausting and they saw very little progress over time, so the songs also helped to boost their morale and keep them going through a long, grueling day.

Since Henry had a steady and increased income

East Texas Research Center Collection

Railroad workers, or "gandy dancers," straighten train rails.

as a railroad worker, perhaps Annie hoped that this move to Anniston would be a chance for change. Maybe she hoped to finally quit working outside her home and instead focus on doing daily chores, taking care of her children, and cooking from scratch several times a day. Unfortunately, this was not the case. To help support her family financially, Annie found it necessary to take on extra work as a laundress for a white family. This was very labor-intensive work. Fortunately, it was work that she could do in her own home, allowing her to at least spend some time with her children while she was working. Annie would likely collect the clothes on a Monday from the family for which she regularly worked. Over the next several days, she would boil the clothes in a large pot of water outside, and then use a washboard to scrub them clean. She then had to rinse, starch, and wring out the clothes, and hang them out to dry. When the clothes were dry, she ironed them using a flat pressing iron heated over fire, or a charcoal iron, being careful not to smudge or burn the clothing. On Saturday she returned the clothing and received a few dollars. She would have to pay for the cost of soap and starch; what was left over went towards necessities for her own family.

Life continued like this for Henry and Annie for several years, being overworked and exhausted from working and providing for their family day after day. We can only speculate as to why, but sometime before 1930, Henry abandoned his family and virtually disappeared, possibly spending some time in the 1940s in Birmingham. Annie must have felt hurt, as well as fearful for the welfare of her family. This trial came at a time, however, when her son, Charles, was prepared to step up as the head of the household at about age

Annie worked as a laundress while living in Anniston, Alabama, much like the woman depicted above.

22. In addition, all of her children worked together to provide for their family. They made sure that their mother did not have to work for another family ever again. Perhaps they had felt the strain on her as she had brought home loads of laundry; perhaps they were making up for what they felt they had missed while growing up. Whatever the reason, they moved to Sylacauga, in Talladega county, Alabama, where each of her children took a job—Charles, David, and Annie Pearl as farm laborers, and John Henry in a shoe shop—and contributed to the household expenses so that Annie could take care of the home.

Over the next few years, three of her four children were married, and John Henry Demps passed away at the young age of 28 from a congenital heart

Margaret Willis Collection

Demps family ca. 1947: Charles, Nellie, Annie Belle, Christine, Charlenia, Charles, Jr., and Margaret

condition. She must have suffered greatly and grieved over the loss of her oldest son, yet Annie's burdens were likely eased by her children, their spouses, and her brand new grandchildren joining the family.

Although Annie had moved to Sylacauga, her thoughts were likely not far from her native Tuskegee. There was too much excitement happening there, and she must have been proud. In 1941 the U.S. Army created the Tuskegee Air Squadron, otherwise known as the Tuskegee Airmen. It was called an "experiment" because the military was unsure of actually allowing African- Americans into the Air Force; many "thought that black men lacked intelligence, skill, courage and patriotism."[2] The first black cadets graduated from the Army Flight School at Tuskegee in 1942, and from 1943 to 1944 these Airmen fought courageously and skillfully in World War II battles throughout North Africa, Sicily, and

Photo courtesy Wikipedia.org

Several of the Tuskegee Airmen in front of a P-40 aircraft during World War II.

Italy. Their courage eventually led to changes that opened the doors to desegregation in the military.

Annie had to be courageous when the time came in 1948 to leave her native Alabama behind to make a new home in the north with her son Charles and his young family. She had lived her life in familiar circumstances, never moving too far away from the farming community where she grew up; now she would be catapulted by train into a new way of life. There were cars everywhere, tall department stores, and boats along the Detroit River. For the next six years, Annie made her home with her son Charles, his wife, Nellie, and their children in a small house on Fleming Street in Detroit. She still did not have to work outside the home, and could spend time with her growing grandchildren. She would never let on, but during this time she began to suffer from serious health problems.

One morning in August of 1954, as she was fin-

From left: Charles Demps, Sr., Nellie Booker Demps, unknown, Annie Pearl Demps, Hattie Brown Demps, David Lee Demps.

ishing her breakfast, Annie quietly had a heart attack and passed away. She left behind a legacy of courage and love, mostly through her children who worked so hard to care for her in return for the care she had given them. She faced many difficult trials and losses, yet she came through them with the support of her family. She taught her children respect and concern for others, a lesson we can all use in our lives today. 🌱

HENRY'S BROTHERS: JAMES, BENJAMIN, LEM, & LUDIE DEMPS

No individual has any right to come into the world and go out of it without leaving something behind.
– George Washington Carver –

UNDERSTANDING the Demps family wouldn't be complete without looking deeper into the lives of Henry Lewis Demps, Jr.'s brothers. Slavery and the Civil Rights Movement most frequently come to mind when thinking about the contributions of African-Americans to our nation's history. However, there were also moments of quiet sacrifice that led to great changes in our country. James, Benjamin, Lem, and Ludie Demps were at the center of some of the most important historical events that happened during their lifetimes, and their lives—as well as the lives of others—were ultimately changed because of their experiences.

James Edward Demps was born in 1888 and was the second surviving child of Henry and Clara Demps. Clara bore several children between the birth of Henry Jr. in 1880 and James in 1888, but sadly, all of those children passed away. James was a blessing and miracle to his parents after several years of heartache. He grew up doing farm labor like his father and brothers, so by 1920 he was married to Louise Byrd, had several small children, and had moved his family in to live with a pair of widowed women while he worked for them as a farm laborer.

Remarkably, James did not remain a farm laborer for much longer. By 1930, he had saved enough money to purchase his own farm, so he worked for himself. He was also supporting a rather large family consisting of his wife and eight children. Unfortunately, despite his economic success, his marriage was failing. In June of 1940, James and Louise were divorced. James didn't wait very long to find a new wife. In November of the same year, he married Annie Belle Howard Pugh. It was Annie who saw James off to war in 1943.

James was one of the first members of the Demps family to serve in the military. On July 28, 1943, near the end of World War II, James E. Demps enlisted as an Apprentice Seaman in the U.S. Navy, and he completed his training at the U.S. Naval Training Center in Great Lakes, Illinois. He was then sent to the U.S. Naval Fuel & Net Depot in Melville, Rhode Island. Finally, James served at the U.S. Naval Air Station in Quonset Point, Rhode Island, where Richard Nixon, who would later become the president of the United States, had completed his naval training just one year earlier.

Even though he completed his basic training, he did not progress very much during the nine months he spent in Rhode Island. He was promoted from Apprentice Seaman to Seaman Second Class, but he did not receive any certificates or special qualifica-

Actual photo of James Edward Demps' graduating class at boot camp.
U.S. Naval Training Station, Great Lakes, Illinois, September 10, 1943.

Photo courtesy Great Lakes Naval Station Museum

tions during his service. Eventually, he was sent home. A disproportionate number of black men, including James, were being "Undesirably Discharged" (also called a "blue discharge" for the paper on which it was printed) during World War II for vague reasons and without being court-martialed. Out of about 48,603 Army blue discharges issued between 1941 and 1945, 10,806 of those (22%) were to black men. Blacks only comprised 6.5% of the Army during that time.[1] These men were not receiving due process of law; they were incriminated by anecdotal evidence, anonymous testimony, or arbitrary offenses. Such offenses included "'character and behavior disorders (the most commonly cited offense),' 'alcoholism,' 'financial irresponsibility...' 'inaptitude,' 'drug addiction,' and 'unsanitary habits' (a common offense rarely cited)."[2]

James was undesirably discharged from the Navy for "Unfitness" on June 29, 1944. Thus, James was likely discharged undesirably for little or no valid reason. The officers above him knew that an other-than-honorable discharge would make employment and other opportunities for success difficult for him for the rest of his life and would keep him from receiving veteran's benefits of any kind. He returned to Tuskegee, where he sought work opportunities, farmed, and lived with his wife, Annie, for the remainder of his life.

* * *

Benjamin Demps was born in 1892. He grew up farming and watching his older brothers work as farm laborers. Perhaps Benjamin also started out working as a farm laborer during his teenage years, but once he had a family he did things a little differently. In 1914, he married Carrie Lou Whitton in Tuskegee, and settled on a rented farm, choosing to labor for himself instead of working as a laborer on someone else's farm. Benjamin and Carrie quickly had two children: Annie Lethia in 1916 and Birdie in 1918. He saved up and was even able to purchase his own farm. Perhaps it seemed to them that life would be relatively easy for their family, until their lives took a terribly tragic turn.

Maybe Benjamin noticed that he was not feeling well. He could have noticed starting to feel sick any-time between 1916 and 1926, first detecting a sore that lasted about three weeks, and then finding red-dish-brown rashes on the palms of his hands and the bottoms of his feet. He may have felt feverish, had a sore throat, patchy hair loss, headaches, weight loss, muscle aches, and fatigue. Benjamin probably thought he just had a bad flu, since hundreds of men in the county were also suffering from the same con-dition. When he finally did seek treatment, the doc-tors told him he had "bad blood." What he really had was syphilis.

Benjamin became "Patient #135," a participant in the Tuskegee Syphilis Study. This study, officially titled "The Tuskegee Study of Untreated Syphilis in the Negro Male," began in 1932 and followed about

Photo courtesy University of Pittsburgh

Health workers traveled around Macon county, testing black men for syphilis and signing them up for the study.

400 African-American men in Macon County, Ala-bama that had previously contracted syphilis. The study was only supposed to have lasted six to eight months. At first there was very little that could be done to treat the condition. They were given mer-cury rubs and bismuth treatments which were slightly effective but highly toxic. After a short time, govern-ment funding ran out and the study was supposed

conclude. But the study was continued when the researchers agreed to make it into a study of untreated syphilis in these men.

The Study participants were still subject then not only to toxic placebo treatments, but to dangerous procedures such as spinal taps, and had to agree to an autopsy after death. The doctors watched them waste away slowly, and published reports on these findings. According to the Centers for Disease Control:

Without treatment, the infected person will continue

Painful, dangerous, non-therapeutic spinal taps were performed on patients as part of the Tuskegee Study.

to have syphilis even though there are no signs or symptoms; infection remains in the body. This latent stage can last for years. The late stages of syphilis can develop in about 15% of people who have not been treated for syphilis, and can appear 10 – 20 years after infection was first acquired. In the late stages of syphilis, the disease may subsequently damage the internal organs, including the brain, nerves, eyes, heart, blood vessels, liver, bones, and joints. Signs and symptoms of the late stage of syphilis include difficulty coordinating muscle movements, paralysis, numbness, gradual blindness, and dementia. This damage may be serious enough to cause death.[3]

In other words, they told the men that they were receiving the best care available, when in fact they were watching them die. Benjamin Demps suffered immensely while under observation, as his condition worsened and he moved into the final stage of the disease. His heart muscles were slowly degenerating, causing serious deterioration of his spleen and kidneys. Eventually, he had an aneurysm in his heart and died. Benjamin was among the first to die during the study, in 1936, only four years after it began.

This study continued, despite its grossly inhumane treatment of hundreds of black men, for 40 years. Men involved in the study were denied treatment with penicillin even after it became widely available in the 1940s. Their names were kept on lists and tracked by health departments wherever they went. Even the military agreed to leave enlisted and drafted soldiers untreated, despite treatment of syphilis being required for everyone else to join the military.[4]

Finally, in 1972, an Associated Press reporter made the story front-page news, which quickly led to change. This study led to government legislation protecting patients from exploitation in biomedical research, requirements of ethical treatment of patients in clinical studies, and mandatory informed consent. In addition, former president Bill Clinton issued an official

Death certificate of Benjamin Demps, showing the complete deterioration of his organ systems as caused by syphilis.
(Courtesy of the Family History Library, on microfilm)

apology for the Tuskegee Experiment on behalf of the U.S. government:

> The United States government did something that was wrong, deeply, profoundly, morally wrong. To the survivors, to the wives and family members, the children and the grandchildren, I say what you know: No power on earth can give you back the lives lost, the pain suffered, the years of internal torment and anguish. What was done cannot be undone. But we can end the silence. We can stop turning our heads away. We can look at you in the eye and finally say on behalf of the American people, what the United States government did was shameful, and I am sorry.[5]

Even though he was not alive to see the day when the experiment ended and an apology finally made, Benjamin Demps will always be remembered, alongside hundreds of other participants, in a memorial constructed in Tuskegee, Alabama to honor them.

*   *   *

Lem was the fourth son of Henry and Clara Demps and was born in 1895. By 1910, he had joined his family working as a farm laborer. He met a young woman named Charlena Mitchell, and they were married in La Place on August 4, 1916. Like his other brothers, Lem was not one to stay settled working as a farm laborer for another family for the rest of his life. Even though it meant leaving home and uprooting his new family, he could not pass up a great opportunity when it came along. In 1917, Lem moved to Anniston, Alabama to work for the L&N Railroad Company along with his brother, Henry. When he registered for the draft during World War I, which every male born between 1872 and 1900 was required to do, he listed his employment as a "track man," another name for the same work that Henry was performing. Fortunately, Lem was not drafted, but his employment situation at the railroad was not as long-lived as he supposed, so by 1920 Lem and Charlena were back in Macon County, farming just a few houses away from Lem's brother, James.

Sometime between 1920 and 1927, Lem and

Charlena's marriage fell apart. They divorced and by 1927, when Lem was 32 years old, he married a young lady named Sadie who was only 17. In 1930 they made heir home in Birmingham, Alabama, where Lem was working as a laborer in a pipe shop.

It is not evident whether Sadie traveled with him,

World War I Draft Registration Card of Lem Demps. Lists his current residence, occupation, marital status, and physical description. (Courtesy of Ancestry.com)

but eventually Lem picked up and moved away to Illinois as part of the second wave of the Great Migration. Lem stayed in Illinois long enough to establish employment, register for Social Security, and gain the skills that would take him into the next phase of his life.

While most people who were leaving the South traveled north and stayed there for the rest of their lives to raise their families, Lem soon headed west to California, where there was a sudden explosion of African-Americans. Much of the work available was at aircraft plants and shipyards along the Pacific coast, where vessels were being built during World War II.[6] The work and the pay were much better, and even though there was still racism, it was not as deeply oppressive as it had been in the South. Lem remained in California for the rest of his life, finally settling in Sacramento. This was a significant accomplishment for someone who grew up in Macon County; somehow he had found enough motivation and hope to leave the place where he was raised and move across the country to a world that was unknown to him. He lived to age 71.

*   *   *

The last of the Demps brothers, Ludie, was born in 1896. Ludie spent most of his years growing up working as a farm hand in La Place. In 1918 he worked as a hired hand on the farm of W.D. Carr, just a few doors down from his parents. Unlike his brothers, Ludie never left his parents' home to seek work in another place. He lived with them through the passing of his father sometime before 1930, and then remained with his mother until 1933. It was then that Ludie was sent 197 miles away to Mobile, Alabama to a hospital at the relatively young age of 34.

Ludie was sent to Searcy Hospital, which was converted from the Mount Vernon military arsenal and barracks into a mental institution in 1900. It was one of the few mental health facilities serving

The Mount Vernon Arsenal barracks became Searcy Hospital, pictured here two years after Ludie arrived.

only African-Americans, until 1969 when it was finally desegregated.[7] We can only speculate as to the difficulties that Ludie suffered during the many years he was institutionalized. There were increasing numbers of people being admitted to mental institutions in the early 1900s, all the way through the 1930s. Many institutions had not yet developed criteria for accepting or rejecting patients, so the reasons for such admissions were varied, from homelessness to old age, to "lunacy," which was behavior interpreted as dangerous, foolish, or unpredictable.

Before Ludie was committed he never left home and never married, so it is likely that he had always had the mental condition, as well as a possible heart defect. The mental condition was probably severe enough that he was not able to function without the help of his family, and it became too great a burden for his mother to care for him in the later years of her life. It is also likely that Ludie could only work as a farm worker because of the physical and emotional limitations that these trials placed on him and his family.

Mental hospitals became overcrowded during the time Ludie was institutionalized, and the level of patient care deteriorated across the country. Patients were starved, drugged into sedation, forced to sleep in restraints and rickety cots, and regularly beaten.[8] In the 1930s lobotomies were introduced as a

"therapy," in addition to the already common practice of electroshock therapy, and routine sterilizations were administered in many states so that peo-

Death certificate of Ludie Demps, showing that he spent more than 32 years–about half of his life–in a mental hospital. (Courtesy of the Alabama Center for Health Statistics)

ple with mental illnesses could not reproduce.[9] Ludie spent 32 years in that facility, and finally died in 1966 of a heart insufficiency, with "mental condition" listed as a contributing factor on his death certificate. As a result of the terrible conditions witnessed and reported during the time Ludie was in a mental hospital, many health policies changed to give more humane, recovery-focused care to individuals suffering from mental illness.

James, Benjamin, Lem, and Ludie Demps represent so many of the sacrifices that African-Americans made and the hardships they endured as America went through a time of growth in technological and medical knowledge. Black men and women are just as much an integral part of this nation's history as any other group of people who came to this country, but often these stories are lost and forgotten. These brothers lived relatively different lives, but they all stand as examples that each of us has our own story, and we each fit into the history of the time in which we are living. It is up to us to make the most of the circumstances present in our lives.✾

HENRY DEMPS, SR. & CLARA LEWIS

*Racism is not an excuse
not to do the best you can.
– Arthur Ashe –*

ENRY Demps, Sr. was born in South Carolina in 1855. He surely had many of the same experiences as other little children his age growing up in the farming community of Marion County, near Mars Bluff: helping his father, John, work the crops as soon as he was old enough; assisting his mother, Mary, with daily chores; and picking on and playing with his younger sister, Malisa. Something was very different about Henry's experience, however, which likely had a deep impact on his life: he was born free in one of the largest slaveholding states in the nation, six years before the Civil War started.

The earliest record of Henry Demps, Sr. is in the

Henry helped on his father's farm as soon as he was old enough, like the boy pictured above.

1860 census with his family, just before South Carolina seceded from the Union and the Civil War began. As Henry grew up, he was constantly reminded of the war going on around him. Not only was the war a subject adults around him must have frequently discussed, but his hometown was also at the center of the Confederate war strategy. Mars Bluff became the site of the only inland Confederate naval yard in South Carolina because of it's location on the Pee Dee River and proximity to the railroad.

Unfortunately, there is no record of Henry and his family in the 1870 census, so we can only speculate as to how and when Henry left South Carolina and ended up in Alabama.

Courtesy LIFE Magazine Online

Shortly after slavery ended, there was a labor surplus in some of the larger slaveholding states such as South Carolina and Virginia, and there was a labor shortage in the Deep South, so many African-Americans migrated there to try to find work. One interesting migration trend is that many Dempses moved from South Carolina to northern Florida. On the 1860 census, there are only two families in South Carolina with the surname Demps; one of them is Henry Demps' family, and the other family lives close by, so they are likely related. Another Demps family lived in North Carolina whose head of household was born in South Carolina. All of these families lived as free colored people during slavery. In 1870, there were several more Demps families listed in South Carolina (presumably because they had been emancipated from slavery), but there were also Demps families in Florida whose birthplaces are listed as South Carolina. These families likely have some connection to our ancestors.

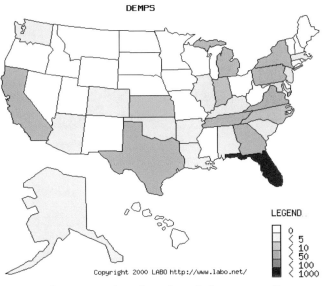

Map showing number of people with the surname Demps in each state as of 2000.

Sometime before 1878, Henry Demps arrived in Macon county, Alabama. Perhaps Henry moved to Alabama to find more work and make a better life for himself than he could have in South Carolina, but circumstances in Macon county were not much better after slavery ended. Even though the end of slavery brought the prospect and hope of freedom to the large population of African-Americans living in the county, the ideal of freedom and the reality of living in the South were very different.

Around the time that Henry Demps arrived in Alabama, just a few years after the end of slavery, many changes were taking place in the United States government. This gave a sense of hope to blacks living in the South that there would be real changes in social interactions with whites and in the inequality they faced in their lifestyles. In 1868, the Fourteenth Amendment was ratified, granting full citizenship to all persons born or naturalized in the United States. Just two years later, the Fifteenth Amendment was added to the Constitution, guaranteeing all men, including African-American men, the right to vote. Unfortunately, both of these rights were largely undermined and ignored throughout the South, as African-Americans were continually treated as lesser citizens. Living in Macon county, Alabama, surely

Henry felt the sting of this unequal treatment as he struggled to make ends meet, or when, as a grown man, he was addressed as "boy" by white men very much his juniors.

Despite all the difficulties Henry faced, he still found happiness for himself and hope for the future when he met Clara Lewis. They were married on January 1st, 1878, and they settled together in Cross

Marriage license of Henry Demps and Clara Lewis, Jan. 1st, 1878. (Courtesy of Macon County Clerk)

Keys, Macon County, Alabama.

Clara worked along side her husband throughout her life. Soon after their marriage, Clara gave birth to their first child, Henry Lewis, in 1880. Perhaps this had been a particularly difficult pregnancy and labor, because Clara had a "nurse" or a young girl staying with their family to help her take care of the new baby. The arrival of their first son surely brought an increased sense of hope to their family.

Just after Henry and Clara welcomed their first son into their family, the nearby town of Tuskegee welcomed a young man named Booker T. Washington to the area who came to open an institute of higher learning for African-Americans in 1881. There were

few opportunities to receive a good education in the community, and many hoped that the establishment of the Tuskegee Institute would be the ticket to their escape from the grasp of poverty.

By 1888 the Tuskegee Institute was flourishing and many students were learning trades and skills such as farming, carpentry, and domestic sciences such as canning. But these students came from families that already had the means to send them to school. I can imagine children in Cross Keys sitting

Photo courtesy Wikipedia.org

"*Tuskegee Normal an*

in their one-room schoolhouses, the wooden planks rotting away from the nails holding them together from years of being pelted by wind and rain. They might have daydreamed about walking around the campus of the Tuskegee Institute, boys dressed in shirts and ties, the girls' hair done up in buns and wearing pretty blue aprons. They thought excitedly about taking classes on the wonders of the peanut from George Washington Carver. But most parents could not afford that path for their children, includ-

Tuskegee Normal and Industrial Institute, which later became Tuskegee University, ca. 1916.

ing Henry and Clara, so they did the best they could to encourage their children to better themselves in whatever ways they could.

It was in 1888 that Henry and Clara welcomed their second surviving child, James, into their family. Clara had given birth to other children after Henry Lewis, but none of them survived. She was plagued with the trial of bearing several more stillborn children throughout her life. By 1900, she had borne 10 children, but only her five sons—Henry, James, Benjamin, Lem, and Ludie—survived.

Just at this time of great struggle for the Demps family, tensions were rising between blacks and whites throughout the South. Lynchings were happening all across the southern states, and in 1895, the terror hit close to home. In Tuskegee, John M. Alexander was lynched accidentally by a group of white men who were seeking to take the life of "Tom Harris, a notorious mulatto man, negro lawyer and rather a seditious character, who had against Mr. Alexander's orders taken refuge within his gates from a pursuing mob."[1] Less than a year later, the Supreme Court decided the *Plessy v. Ferguson* case—that segregation and Jim Crow laws did not conflict with thirteenth and fourteenth amendment rights, establishing the "separate but equal" precedent. It seems that all of the progress blacks fought for was systematically being taken away.

Around 1900, Henry decided to move his family a short distance to La Place, just eight doors down from Clara's mother and stepfather, Argentine and Richard Scott. Argin and Richard were married in 1871, and they spent most of their lives together farming in La Place. In 1907, Richard and Argin moved from La Place to the Tuskegee Institute when they made a rather remarkable purchase. Somehow they had managed to save up $600 to buy a three-room house and surrounding lot on Washington Avenue from Booker T. Washington himself! He and his wife, Margaret Washington, were already living in the historic Oaks home, so they were able to sell this prop-

Richard Scott purchased a house and land from Booker T. and Maggie Washington in September of 1907. (Courtesy of Macon County Clerk)

erty to Clara's mother and step-father. They were living in the midst of the action of the prestigious Tuskegee Institute. This situation lasted only for a short time, though; by 1920, Richard was renting farm land again in La Place and had remarried. Argin had either left him or more likely had passed away.

Clara's father, Alfred W. Lewis, also stayed close by her throughout most of her life. He was a hard worker, and in 1902 became the first person in the family to own land. Alfred also had a home that was open to others who were in need. He often had nieces, nephews, and cousins living with him when they needed a place to stay, and he looked after his aging mother, Harriet Fort Lewis, for almost three decades until she passed away at 92.

With extended family as examples, Henry worked hard to raise five sons and to save what money he could. In 1908, Henry Demps, Sr. became a landowner. With only eighty-five dollars, he was able to buy seven acres of land in La Place, which is now known as Shorter, in Macon County, Alabama.

This piece of land is located near the current location of Cole Cemetery, where several members of the Demps family and other ancestors are buried. The land was also bounded on the east by what was formerly known as Simmons road; many of the gravestones that are still intact bear the Simmons surname. Unfortunately, the cemetery is very overgrown, and relatively few of the stones are readable. One of the few stones that is still standing is that of Clara's grandmother, Hattie Fort

MOTHER Hattie Lewis, Born Jan. 14, 1814, Died Nov. 6 1906. "Rest, mother, rest in quiet sleep while friends in sorrow oer thee weep."

Kristen Andersen Collection

Lewis. She died in 1906, so the stone had been preserved for over 100 years by the time we found it. Witnessing the state of the other grave markers in the cemetery, it was nothing short of a miracle.

Of the stones that are still standing, most of them are inscribed with symbols of the Freemasons. This was very interesting, because at first thought, Freemasonry does not seem synonymous with African-American life. But Booker T. Washington, who lived in Tuskegee from 1881 to 1915 and was very influential in the community, was also a Freemason. Further research reveals that there have been many other successful black Freemasons, such as Thurgood Marshall, W.E.B. DuBois, Nat 'King' Cole, Duke Ellington, and Jesse Jackson.[3]

The first black Masonic Lodge in Macon County was established and purchased land shortly before Henry Demps bought his seven acres, and it seems as though the black Freemason community in Macon County flourished during this time. Even today, the

Photo courtesy Archives of Ontario

Black Freemasons ready for a meeting

largest number of black Freemasons in the U.S. resides in Alabama.[4] The fact that many African-American Freemasons were buried in the Cole Cemetery, so very close to Henry Demps, Sr.'s land and where his wife, son, and other family members are buried, suggests that he lived in very close proximity with many of them. It also presents the possibility that he was a Freemason himself.

Henry and Clara Demps continued to work together to support their family for many years, until around 1930, when Henry passed away. Clara continued to care for her mentally challenged son, Ludie, for a few more years, until she was old enough that she couldn't effectively care for him alone anymore. She lived out the rest of her life in Tuskegee.

In such turbulent times, when rights were threatened at every turn, our ancestors still worked hard to be smart, successful, and to participate in the social discourse where they lived. They labored to take care of their families and help them to attain better circumstances for their lives. They saw the extreme importance of bettering their circumstances and working to achieve their dreams. Their risks to live better lives are examples to us as we take risks in our own lives to fulfill our potential and become who we truly deserve to be. ✤

JOHN DEMPS

I had crossed the line. I was free; but there was no one to welcome me to the land of freedom. I was a stranger in a strange land.
—Harriet Tubman—

JOHN Demps represents all of the amazement and self-discovery that comes from researching one's family history. His is a story that is full of meaning but that was lost as our ancestors struggled daily just to survive. Born in 1837 in South Carolina, John Demps grew up in one of the most fervent slave states in America. But John Demps had a fate that was different from many other colored people at the time: he was one of the relatively few who lived free during slavery.

In 1850, John was 12 years old and was living with another free colored family, the Hunts, in Marlborough, South Carolina. Living nearby was Peter Demps, age 54, a free black man who was also born in South Carolina. Peter was employed at the time as a "Ferryman," so it is very possible that they lived near the Great Pee Dee River that ran through Marlboro and Marion counties. The river was named after the Pee Dee Indian tribe that lived along the river, and was established during colonial times as an important trade route for the exportation of lumber and rice. Peter's work would have consisted of transporting people and their goods from one side of the river to the other. Ferries were very simple in the mid - to late-1800s: they were much like a wooden bridge that had no attachment to the shore, so people could step onto the ferry, and the ferryman could float it back and forth across the river. Running the ferry would have been very good

Ferry on the Pee Dee River

work for a free black man living in rural South Carolina at that time.

It is highly likely that Peter Demps is John's father, but because they are not living in the same household, it is not possible to prove it by the surnames alone. One possible explanation is that John's mother had passed away, and instead of leaving him to grow up without a mother, the nearby Hunt family took him in. Lydia Hunt was a single mother of five children, and having a twelve-year-old boy to help out with farm work and other chores would have been a mutually beneficial situation. John would have a mother figure and could still live near his father, while being able to earn his keep.

Being a free colored person before the end of slavery was an incredible challenge, especially in South Carolina. In this particular state, it was illegal for free blacks to be taught to read and write, just as

1850 US census listing John Demps and Peter Demps, both colored, as "Free Inhabitants" of Marlboro, SC. (Courtesy of Ancestry.com)

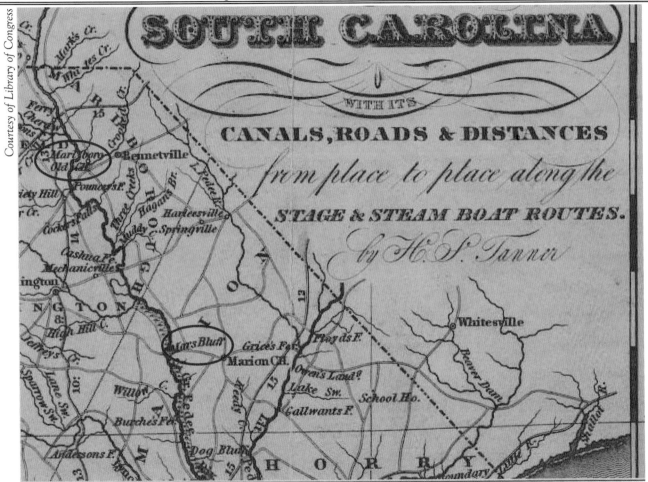

Map of South Carolina published in 1833; red circles denote the locations where John Demps lived.

Page No. 57

SCHEDULE 1.—Free Inhabitants in *Marion* in the County of *Marion* State of *So. Ca.* enumerated by me, on the 22nd day of *June* 1860. *H. W. Williams* Ass't Marshal. Post Office *Mars Bluff, So. Ca.*

it was illegal to teach these skills to slaves. Thus, John Demps never became literate, which was so important to becoming completely self-sufficient. "Freedom" ensured very few additional rights for free colored people because white slave owners were still the lawmakers. In fact, in 1860, the state legislature attempted to pass legislation to enslave even the free blacks in the state. Fortunately, the Civil War began in 1861, so the focus was shifted away from this matter and the plan was abandoned. [1]

Not only was John Demps a free person of color, but on census records he and his family were all listed as "mulatto," or of mixed race, which means that they were forced into a particularly difficult role in society. In addition to being hated by white people for not being slaves, mulattos were hated by them for being part white. The slightest comment could be construed as acting "uppity" and

1860 US census in South Carolina listing John Demps and his family. He was one of the wealthiest men in the area, yet he remained illiterate. (Courtesy of Ancestry.com)

could be cause for violence. Surprisingly, though, interracial marriage was not illegal in South Carolina until 1890.[2] In the 1830s and 1840s, there were several Dempseys in South Carolina who were free black men married to white women (which was not uncommon in South Carolina at the time), and mulatto children born to white women were considered free.[3] This is one possibility of how the Demps surname originated, and how John was able to be born as a free person of color in such an unforgiving time period.

Despite the challenges he had to confront, John Demps was still able to provide for himself and his family. By 1860 he had moved to Mars Bluff in Marion County, South Carolina, married his sweetheart, Mary, and was the father of two children, Henry and Malisa. John rented land and tended it as a farmer like most colored men did in his situation. However, unlike most other men in his situation, John was extremely prosperous. An assessment of the 1860 census reveals that John's personal assets total $2100; this amounts to several times more than the assets of almost all of his neighbors. Furthermore, John's family is the only colored family listed on the entire census page. Not only were they the only colored family, but they were also one of the wealthiest in the neighborhood. He accomplished all of this without being able to read or write. Whether he earned this money through his farming, inherited it from his father Peter's ferry boat business, or both, he was successful and a very unique member of society in Marion county.

Although we do know that John's son, Henry Demps, arrived safely in Alabama sometime before 1878, it is unclear what happened to John, Mary, and Malisa Demps after 1860. There are several possibilities. South Carolina was the first state to secede from the Union, which eventually led to the Civil War in 1861. First, they could have been killed in the violence that took place during the war, whether

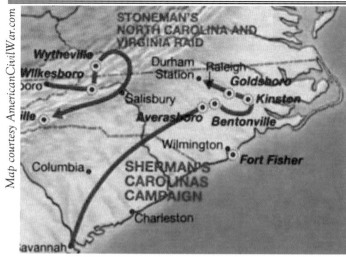

Pathway followed by Sherman's army from Bamberg County, SC, through Marion County, SC, to Lenoir County, NC during the Carolinas Campaign.

in South Carolina or while fleeing elsewhere for safety. Mars Bluff was the site of a Confederate Naval Yard, where they constructed ships to be used in battle during the Civil War. In March of 1865, 500 Federal soldiers from Indiana marched into Marion county to destroy the railroad depot and cut off supplies and communication to the Confederate hold-

ing at Mars Bluff, an altercation now known as the Skirmish at Gamble's Hotel. In addition, there was fear among the Confederate soldiers at the Mars Bluff Naval Yard of General William Sherman and his "Campaign of the Carolinas," during which several battles took place as Sherman's army moved northward between Georgia and North Carolina, destroying nearly everything in its path. Out of fear that their gunboat, the CSS Pee Dee, would be captured by Sherman's army, the Confederate soldiers at Mars Bluff threw the cannons overboard and set the boat on fire.[4] It is possible that there were civilian casualties during these battles in and around Mars Bluff, including John and his family.

Another possible reason that John, Mary, and Malisa seem to have disappeared is that they could have died because of disease, which was not uncommon in the mid-1800s. People frequently died of causes that are often treatable today, such as pneumonia, dysentery, "dropsy" (edema or excessive water retention due to heart or kidney problems), or during childbirth. It also seems, according to the 1860 census, that people in Marion county were dying of typhoid fever, likely due to contaminated drinking water and unsanitary conditions. There were no antibiotics or vaccinations for typhoid such as are available today, and complications could develop as a result of the illness that could also contribute to premature death.

Another possibility is that John, Mary, and Malisa left the South to start a different life for themselves in the north—passing for white. On the 1850 census, John Demps and the Hunt family with whom he was living are all listed as mulatto. In 1860, however, none of the Hunts are listed as mulatto; they are all listed as white. In fact, the daughters of Lydia Hunt all had spouses who are white, so they continued to be listed as such throughout their lives. Perhaps John, Mary, and Malisa were light-skinned enough to pass for white, and they parted ways with

Henry during the 1860s or 1870s to move north, change their names, and start over with a new existence. Henry may not have been light enough to pass with them, and so he would have had to cut off contact with his family completely. That could also explain why the history of this family was lost.

Assuming that Peter Demps is the father of John Demps, then our story begins with him, born in 1796, working as a free black man in South Carolina. How the Dempses became free is still yet to be determined, but their freedom during a tumultuous time is something that we can cherish. We can be proud of their sacrifices and successes while living among people who plotted to enslave them. Today we can appreciate the level of freedom that we enjoy, and we can make choices to use our freedom to improve life for ourselves, our children, and those around us. As we rediscover and embrace the stories of our ancestors, previously lost and forgotten, it changes the context of who we know ourselves to be. ⚜

SECTION TWO:

Booker

NELLIE MAE BOOKER

*The true worth of a race must be measured
by the character of its womanhood.*
–Mary McLeod Bethune–

Margaret Willis Collection

Nellie Booker Demps

ELLIE Mae Booker spent a large portion of her life caring for others. Born in May of 1913, she was the oldest surviving girl of eight children. Nellie grew up learning all of the responsibilities of homemaking that her mother and grandmothers already knew: cooking, tending farm animals, growing vegetables, quilting, and taking care of her younger brothers and sisters. Everything she learned from her mother helped her with her family responsibilities throughout her life, even when they came earlier than she expected.

When her mother passed away at the young age of 34, Nellie was only 15 years old. She was previously in school, but had to take time away to become a "home keeper."[1] She had to grow up quickly and take on the responsibility of becoming the woman of the house for a time. She did have the help of her grandparents, Es and Fannie Estell, who moved next door to help look after the family. The passing of her mother just as she was coming into her teenage years, at the time when she would have wanted her around the most, was a tremendous loss.

Despite these difficulties, Nellie drew strength in being with her family. She lived very close to both her maternal and paternal grandparents, and grew to love them very much. She especially grew to appreciate the land that her grandfather, Sherman Booker, worked so hard to secure, and she clung to that land for the rest of her life. Nellie also lived near many of her aunts, uncles, and cousins, as well as people with whom she attended church, so she had a large network of extended family and friends. As Nellie grew older she kept small books filled with names, addresses, and phone numbers of people with whom she communicated over the years, especially through letters and cards.

Throughout her life, Nellie was a woman of faith, and this faith was instilled in her even as a child. Nellie loved the Lord and she loved to sing spirituals about him. She was baptized at the Mount Olive Baptist Church in Sycamore, Alabama, and several generations of her family before her had attended that same church. It was after church one Sunday early in the spring of 1933 that Nellie and her friends noticed a handsome young man wearing a hat, looking intently in their direction.

"Nellie, he's looking at you!" her friends whispered excitedly.

"No he's not, he's looking at you," she replied, glancing back at him to see if he really was looking at her. Her eyes met his, and he smiled.

"He's coming this way!" Nellie's friends giggled. They smoothed their hair and their dresses and pretended not to see him coming. He approached Nellie directly.

Kristen Andersen Collection

Mount Olive Baptist Church in 2007, recently rebuilt.

"Hello, miss," he said, tipping his hat. He did not take his eyes off of her. She returned the greeting and he asked for her name; he said that his name was Charles Demps, and that he would like to see her again.[2]

He did see her again. And on December 17, 1933, Charles William Demps and Nellie Mae Booker were married at her father's home in Sycamore, Alabama. Charles and Nellie made their home in nearby Sylacauga, where Charles was working, and by 1935 they built their first home and had their own land to farm. Nellie's hard work and care for others continued throughout her married life as she supported her husband and began to raise children. Their first daughter, Christine, arrived less than one year after they were married, in November 1934. Two years later, twins Charles

Charles and Nellie Demps

and Charlenia arrived, and in 1938 their fourth child, Margaret, joined them. Nellie cared for these children while assisting Charles with the farm work.

In 1946, when Charles went north to work for Chrysler until he could save enough money to send for the rest of the family, Nellie took over the work on the farm. Each day she would arise early in the morning to milk the cow and churn fresh butter. She gathered eggs from the hens and fed the chickens. She prepared breakfast for her children before they went off to school for the day, because it was important for them to have a good meal so they could concentrate on their studies. Nellie would grab the pitchfork to bring hay down from the loft in the barn to feed the horse, and sometimes a snake would come down along with it. Without hesitation, she would spear the snake with the pitch-

Margaret Willis Collection

THIS CERTIFIES

THAT

Mr. Thos Demps

of Sylacauga

State of Alabama

AND

Miss Nellie Booker

of of Talladega

State of Alabama

Were United in

Holy Matrimony

At The home of J. Booker According to the Ordinance of God and the Laws of the
State of Alabama on the 17 th day of December 1933

John Millender
George Sawler
and a host of other
friends

J. M. Swain

Far left: Larry Demps. Center photo, left to right: Charles, Jr.; Charlenia; Margaret; Christine; and Nellie Demps, at their home in Sylacauga, AL. Far right: Gary Demps.

fork or just stomp on it with her foot and continue with her duties. She had no time for fear; she had too much work to do. There were fields to plow or crops to harvest, cotton to pick, laundry to wash by hand, children to welcome home and encourage in doing their chores, and dinner to make from scratch. And at the end of the day, when the children were in bed, Nellie would relax by cutting up old dresses and hand stitching them into beautiful quilts. When I visited Grandma on her 90th birthday, she told me the secret to her longevity. "Baby," she sighed, "I'm 90 years old, and I worked *so* hard."

Nellie's work did not end there. She made certain that her home was open to people who were less fortunate than her and her family. After Charles established himself working for Chrysler in Detroit,

Michigan, Nellie moved with the rest of the family to Detroit in 1948. There was a time shortly after their arrival when some of Charles' cousins needed a place to stay for a while. They were immediately made welcome in Nellie's home. Christine, Charlenia, Charles Jr., and Marie all had to squeeze into one bed, two heads at each end, with their feet in each other's faces, so their extended family would have beds to sleep in during their stay. Even though they were uncomfortable, they learned about sharing what they had with others in need, especially family.

Nellie continued to care for others even as she welcomed her last two sons, Larry and Gary, in to the family in 1949 and 1952, respectively. Besides those who stayed with them for short periods of time, for many years her mother-in-law, Annie Magruder Demps, lived in her home as well. Charles had been the head of household in his mother's home since his father left in the 1920s, and when he moved his wife and children to Michigan, his mother

---

Alzheimer's Disease: A Curse and A Blessing

I felt sad when I realized that Grandma was suffering from Alzheimer's disease and that her short-term memory was becoming increasingly limited. It was difficult to answer the same few questions over and over, knowing that I would have to answer them again in a few minutes. Undoubtedly this must have been an even greater challenge to those who visited and cared for her more frequently.

I was amazed, however, at Grandma's incredibly sharp long-term memory. She recalled her first meeting with Grandpa with vivid clarity, and remembered details about the church she attended as a child. She never forgot the face of her "daddy," Joe Booker. In the last few months of her life, the "filter" that allowed her to bite her tongue all her life essentially dissolved and she said some things about Grandpa that, although not terribly surprising to hear, were shocking coming from my 94-year-old grandmother. It was as if she finally had a chance to say all of the things it had never been "appropriate" for her to say before, but without any control over it or any consequences.

As much as her Alzheimer's was a challenge to others and was surely a difficult way for her to spend her final years, perhaps in some way she was able to get some things out that she never otherwise would have said.

Nellie Demps Collection

Charles and Nellie's 50th wedding anniversary party, December 1983. From left to right:
Top: Gary Demps, Name unknown, Matthew Curry, Charles Demps III, Unknown Hawkins, Lisa Curry Hawkins, Carol Willis, Margaret Demps Willis, Raymond Willis, Gerald Willis, Thomas Curry, Marilyn Williams, Jane Baringer Demps, Larry Demps. *Middle:* Charles Demps, Jr., Charlenia Demps Curry, Charles Demps, Sr., Nellie Booker Demps, Christine Demps Williams. *Bottom:* Gary Demps, Jr., Kristen Demps, Michael Demps.

came with them. Nellie made it possible for her mother-in-law, Annie, to live comfortably with them until her death in 1954.

It seemed like Nellie's love spread from her home into the neighborhood. Anytime I visited her and Grandpa as a child at their home at 15890 Asbury Park, I felt like Grandma was the most famous woman on the street! Adults, children, and even normally withdrawn teenagers would not pass by without cheerfully greeting her, "Hello, Mrs. Demps." Many would stop on the front steps to chat as Grandma and I sat in green and white woven lawn chairs on the porch. Neighbors looked closely after their home as Nellie and Charles advanced in age, not just out of curiosity but because they truly cared about their well-being.

One of the things that Nellie valued the most was family. I loved the family picture wall that was a permanent fixture in her home since before I was born. She valued relationships and preserving his-

tory, and the picture wall was evidence to me of her passion for preserving both the family history and the love and relationships within the family. Nellie kept her home open to children, grandchildren, nieces, nephews, or cousins stopping by, and somehow she always seemed to have something delicious to offer guests—my absolute favorite was her homemade peach cobbler. Grandma spoke to me with

Visiting Grandma at the nursing home, February 2007.

Kristen Andersen Collection

love about everyone in the family—people who were living or who had passed on, people who came to visit or those she wished she saw more often. Even as her Alzheimer's disease progressed, her constant concern was still about family. Shortly after I came home from my missionary service in Madagascar, Grandma must have decided it was time to talk to me about having my own family.

"Child, when are you gonna have me some grandbabies?"

"I don't know, Grandma. I have to get married first!" I thought I could get out of answering the question, hoping that she would drop the subject. But with Alzheimer's, it came back up every ten minutes.

After I got married, when I brought my husband to visit, I could tell that the disease had progressed, because every four or five minutes she would need a reminder about who Jon was. Several moments of confused staring would be my cue to show her my wedding ring again. "Grandma, that's my husband, Jon."

She would gasp in surprise every time. "That's your husband? He's *cute*! Now when are you all gonna have me some grandbabies?"

I love Grandma with my whole heart. She was gentle with me in a way that I felt no one else in the world was. Sometimes she would sit me on her lap, let down my hair, and sing me spirituals, giving me a connection to truth that I needed so very much in my life. As I got older, she was open and honest with me about important events that impacted my family. She wasn't afraid to be bold, and she wasn't afraid of the truth. She cared for me, and she cared for others. Nellie Mae Booker Demps is an example of charity, hard work, and valuing family. I miss her dearly, and I look forward to seeing her again someday. ❦

JOE BOOKER

I am what time, circumstance, history, have made of me, certainly,
but I am also much more than that. So are we all.
—James Baldwin—

J SAT in the LaGuardia airport in New York a few years ago, not even thirty minutes from where my great-grandfather, Joe Booker, lived during the last years of his life. Because of the heavy mid-day traffic, my layover was not quite long enough to catch a cab to visit his old apartment on West 144th Street in Harlem, or even to visit his grave at the Fair Lawn Cemetery in Bergen County, New Jersey. I was disappointed, yet again feeling like the possibility of connecting to some aspect of Joe Booker's life rested outside of my reach. He remained a mystery to me.

Over and over, I have encountered stumbling blocks as I have researched Joe Booker's life. Very few people I have talked to know anything about him, and the few that do have information

Joe Booker in Detroit,
January 1964

know virtually nothing about his life after he moved away from the South and settled in New York. Even the census, which has been my most reliable resource, is missing the page in 1910 that should include him, his wife, Josie, and their newborn daughter, Margie Estella. Those who knew Joe Booker personally were either too young to know the details about his personal life, are now too old to remember, or have already passed away. I have therefore been left to search public records to decipher the mystery behind my great-grandfather's life.

Joseph Booker, known throughout his life as Joe, was born in 1887, the first of ten children born to Sherman and Callie Booker. Even his name is surrounded in mystery: several family members relate that he had a middle name, Hannibal, but there is no record that he used this middle name or that his parents gave him this name. Joe's family lived next to the family after whom Ledbetter Flat Road in Talladega County is named and from whom they likely rented their land. As he grew older, Joe learned the farming trade from his father and worked as a farm hand for various planters in the community. In addition, he was fortunate to learn the difficult but useful skills of blacksmithing alongside his brothers Willie, Thomas B., and Booker T. They were most likely able to use their skills at the nearby Jemison Plantation, where there was a sizeable horse farm; this may also be where they learned the skills of shoeing horses and working with iron. At one point, the brothers even had their own business running a blacksmith shop.[1]

It was not long before tall, handsome Joe found a young lady who caught his eye. He married Josie Estell in 1908, and set out to provide for his new family. Working as a farm laborer was not always reliable, but it was the best job that most people could get. Like many people at the time, Joe found himself unable to provide for his family without incurring some debt. In 1911, he had to mortgage

Joe had to mortgage "One...mare mule about 6 years old name[d] Ada" and "one open top buggy" for his family to survive. (Courtesy of Talladega County Clerk of Probate Court)

Ada, their family mule, and in 1912 he added to that their open-top buggy, all for the sum of one hundred forty dollars. The borrowed money was probably used for rent payment on the land, purchasing a plow, seed, other farming tools, and whatever food his family needed that was not covered by his wages or the farming they did on their own land. Every year the interest increased, and more had to be mortgaged to keep up with the debt.

Fed up with living in a cycle of debt, Joe decided to seek work at the Avondale Cotton Mill in Sycamore. The work was exhausting and paid very little, but it was reliable. White workers could make up to 45 cents per hour working machinery that extracted seeds from the cotton, spun onto bobbins, or woven into cloth. Black workers were usually segregated

Advertisment in The Avondale Sun *ca. 1946. Note that the ad encourages bringing children into the fields. It also mentions white people's increased role in harvesting the crop, but does not depict that image.*
(Courtesy of The Avondale Sun)

and did more janitorial work or picked cotton, and were likely paid less.[2] Whatever work Joe Booker did, it provided him with steady employment, allowed him to take care of his eight children, and provided their family with some added stability.

Stability was exactly what the Booker family needed in 1929, as their lives fell apart with the death of Joe's wife, Josie. She had been by his side for nearly twenty-one years, raising their children, cooking their meals, and providing comfort at the ends of exhausting days in the fields. Suddenly she was gone, and he was left to be a single parent. I believe that this was a turning point in Joe's life, and one from which he never fully recovered.

A Struggling Young Widower

The jury is still out on whether or not Joe Booker ever remarried. I never heard about him having another wife growing up, but there are several records that point to the possibility that he was remarried at least once. In December of 1930, there is a marriage of a Joe Booker to Clare Leonard in Talladega, Alabama. There were many Leonards in the area where the Bookers lived, but only one Joe Booker that I can find, so it would not be a stretch to think that Joe would quickly marry a woman he already knew to help take care of the children. Perhaps this marriage was short-lived, or perhaps it is one of the reasons that all of Joe's sons quickly moved away to Chicago and rarely saw him afterwards. Several of Joe's grandchildren do not remember him visiting Chicago often, if at all, and only visited New York for his funeral.

Joe died unmarried, but that doesn't mean that he did not have other relationships with women. After moving to New York, he supposedly stayed frequently in hotels, and on one of these overnight stays left the only picture of Josie that he had on the night stand. He had two brothers who lived in New York, as well as a daughter, so it seems unusual that he would live in hotels instead of with a family member. His uprooted lifestyle may also have been another cause for some of the difficulty in his relationships with his family.

Perhaps it was not an ideal situation and was hurtful to others, but his possibly unsavory behavior can be better understood when looked at from the perspective of a young widower who lost his dear wife and did not know how else to deal with the pain of it.

Soon after Josie's death, her parents moved next door to help Joe take care of his children and he went back to work at the cotton mill. His brothers William and Thomas had already moved to New York, and his daughter Callie was living with Willie's family. Over the next few years, his children began to marry: first Frank, then Nellie. Soon Frank, Joseph, Pearson, and Richard all moved to Chicago, while Fannie and Georgia ended up in New York with their sister, Callie. Nellie and her family moved to Detroit.

Joe finally left Alabama during the 1940s, following his brothers to New York City. Joe's brothers lived in the heart of Harlem at an exciting yet difficult time in its history. William's family lived just three blocks from the legendary Apollo Theater which opened in 1934. The Savoy Ballroom was also nearby, an integrated venue for music and swing dancing. Despite the entertainment and diversion available throughout the area as well as the cultural

The Savoy Ballroom was an integrated venue where dances such as the Lindy Hop became famous.

Courtesy The Coffey Park Harlem Renaissance website

and political growth, there was also much poverty and violence. Blacks were charged significantly more for housing than whites, sometimes paying more than double the amount for the same space. Many people had to take in lodgers to help share the cost of rent, and sometimes people had "rent parties" where neighbors paid to attend the party to help the host make his or her rent that month, especially during and after the Great Depression. Harlem also saw several riots, usually sparked because of violence by whites toward a black person.

Still, living in Harlem was an escape in many ways from the heavy oppression of living in the south. After slavery ended, Black Codes compelled freed slaves into a second-class status, and later racism became even more openly practiced after the Supreme Court's ruling on *Plessy v. Ferguson*. With the establishment of the "Separate but Equal" legal doctrine, as well as Jim Crow laws, every aspect of life for blacks was affected by segregation, racism, and terrible mistreatment. Even as Joe headed North on a train to escape the oppression of the South, he would have done so in a train car marked "Colored," segregated from the white passengers.

No one seems to know exactly what kind of work Joe did once he arrived in New York, other than that he was a laborer. There was plenty of labor to go around in New York City in the 1930s and 40s, however. Many factories had opened, attracting African-Americans to the area during the Great Migration. Joe's brother, Thomas, worked in a glue factory, and his brother, William, worked in a soap factory. Other family members worked in tailor shops, cleaning office buildings, laying concrete for the growing subway system, or as personal chauffeurs for white families. There was a fruit packing factory, a

Nellie Demps and Joe Booker in Detroit in the 1970s

sugar plant, and even a corset factory.[3] Work opportunities were abundant, and Joe labored diligently until his retirement.

One thing about Joe Booker's life is certain: he made regular trips to Detroit to visit his oldest daughter, Nellie. For several years, his other daughters lived in New York City, so he had to make the eleven-hour drive to Detroit to visit Nellie. Perhaps the additional four hours it would take to drive to Chicago deterred him from visiting his sons very often, but several of his grandchildren from Chicago remember seeing him very little. As he progressed in age, Joe's daughter, Fannie, and her husband, Roland DeWitt, invited him to live with them in their Harlem apartment at 203 W 144th St. He lived out the rest of his days with them there until his passing in April 1980 at the age of 92.

Despite the mysteries of his life, Joe was well-loved. Each time I would show my grandmother Nellie his picture, she would sit tall in her chair and say proudly, "That's my daddy, Joe Booker." Perhaps they had forged a special relationship after Josie passed and Nellie had to step up in her responsibilities as the oldest daughter, or during his later years as he became more frail. Nevertheless, at the end of her life when she struggled through Alzheimer's disease to remember names and faces, Nellie never forgot that she loved her daddy.

I never got to meet "Big Papa," as he was called by his grandchildren. He died just five months before I was born. I wish I could have known this man who still seems like a mystery to so many of us in the family. There is no doubt that he spent his life working hard as a laborer, but at what exact trade, none of us knows. His personal life remains cloaked in the silent graves of the people who knew him, and now all that is left is a paper trail. ✾

WILLIAM SHERMAN BOOKER & CAROLINE JEMISON

There is in this world no such force as [that] of a person determined to rise.
The human soul cannot be permanently chained.
–W.E.B. Dubois –

*W*ILLIAM Sherman Booker was born just six months before the end of slavery, in January of 1865. He grew up during the period of reconstruction following the Civil War, in a time when former slaves were finding their new place in society. For many African-Americans, including Sherman's father, Daniel, sharecropping was the only choice in an attempt to make a living and provide for their families. Sherman grew up watching his father, and then his older brothers, mortgage their property as collateral for loans to rent farm land. As Sherman grew up, he also became a sharecropper, and incurred debt as he started a family and a farm of his own.

In February 1886, Sherman married Caroline Jemison, and by the end of August 1887, they had already welcomed their first son, Joseph, to their family. By February of 1888, Sherman owed $55 to D.L. and J.A. Lewis. As a guarantee that he would pay them back by October of the same year, he mortgaged his "entire crop of corn and cotton, fodder and hay, raised by me or under my supervision, in this harvest year, on the farm I now live or elsewhere."[1] These were difficult terms to manage, and usually this first mortgage was the beginning of a lifetime of debt for a sharecropper.

Yet somehow Sherman was able to pull himself out of this system over time, and in October of 1915 Sherman Booker purchased twenty acres of land in Sycamore, Alabama. This is nothing short of a miracle. What is even more of a miracle is the fact that by 1930, Sherman not only still owned that twenty acres, but had somehow managed to buy more than sixty additional acres of land! Most of this land has been in the family from that time in 1915 until now, although some of the land is being sold off.

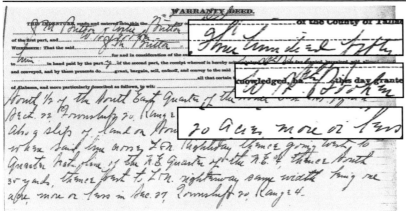

Sherman Booker first purchased 20 acres of land for $350 in Sycamore in 1915. (Courtesy Talladega County Clerk of Probate Court)

It is difficult for me to see a part of our family history that has been preserved for over 90 years leave the family possession. To Sherman, buying the land meant more than just owning property; it is symbolic of our family's escape from a second bondage—the bondage of debt—and stands as a monument to encourage us to escape from anything that might hinder our freedom. It symbolizes Sherman's desire to give something tangible to his family, by which we

can remember his struggle and that of his parents, and so his posterity would never have to go without a place to call home. He was acting as a provider for his entire family, including those of us who had not yet been born. It must have taken great sacrifice to obtain as much land as he did, living in such institutionalized oppression, and I am grateful for the lessons that these sacrifices leave behind for us.

Sherman's wife, Caroline "Callie" Jemison, was born in 1867 in Talladega county to Charles Jemison, but it is still unclear who her mother was. Callie had to live with relatives growing up, possibly because her mother was sick and passed away when she was very young. According to family lore, several of her grandchildren described her as "a mean white lady."[2] She was likely very light-skinned, but she was always listed as black on legal documents. Though it is no excuse for being mean, it is possible that losing her mother and moving between relatives' homes at a young age created a sense of bitterness in her life from which she never fully recovered. We can also assume that she made sacrifices in supporting the family's escape from the sharecropping system, and that perhaps she was hardened by the difficulties that she faced throughout her life.

Callie's father, Charles Jemison, was born around 1842, and was likely owned by the prominent slaveholding Jemison family in Talladega County. This same Jemison family owned the ancestors of Dr. Mae Jemison, a physician, professor, and astronaut, who in 1992 became the first African-American

Red circle on map denotes total area that Sherman Booker owned in Sycamore at one time. (Courtesy of Talladega County Clerk of Probate Court)

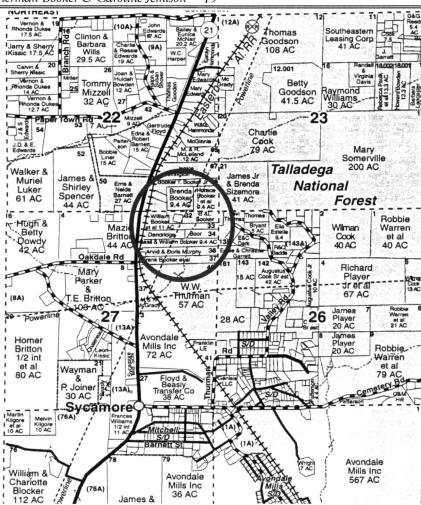

Kristen Andersen collection

Left to right: Edio Gudiel-Teo, Lena Booker Gudiel-Teo, Jon Andersen, Kristen Demps Andersen. Lena still lives on land purchased many years ago by our common ancestor, Sherman Booker.

woman to enter space while serving on the crew of the Space Shuttle *Endeavor*.[3]

The Jemisons became part of history when in 1935 the U.S. government organized the Works Progress Administration (WPA), which provided jobs for many unemployed people during the reconstructive period following the Great Depression. One of the branches of the WPA, the Federal Writer's Project,

concentrated on collecting oral histories of citizens across America, including narratives of former slaves. Among the narratives collected is one belonging to Perry Sid Jemison, a former slave born in Alabama and whose owners are very likely related to the slave-holding Talladega Jemisons.[4][5] His experience is likely very similar to that of our own ancestors on the plantations of Alabama:

De hol entire family lived together on the Cakhoba river, Perry County, Alabama. After dat we wuz scattered about, some God knows where.

...Der wuz no food allowance for chillun that could not work and my grandmother fed us out of her and my mudders allowance. I member my grandmudder giving us pot-licker, bread and red syrup.

De furst work I done to get my food wuz to carry water in de field to de hands dat wuz workin'. De next work after dat, wuz when I wuz large enough to plow. Den I done eberything else that come to mind on de farm. I neber earned money in dem slave days.

Your general food wuz such as sweet potatoes, peas and turnip greens. Den we would jump out and ketch a coon or possum. We ate rabbits, squirrels, ground-hog and hog meat. We had fish, catfish and scale fish. Such things as greens, we boil dem. Fish we fry. Possum we parboil den pick him up and bake him. Of all dat meat I prefar fish and rabbit. When it come to vegetables, cabbage wuz my delight, and turnips. De slaves had their own garden patch...

My massa wuz named Sam Jemison and his wife wuz named Chloe....Dey hed 750 acres on de plantation.... Der wuz bout 60 slaves on de plantation. Dey work hard and late at night. Dey tole me dey were up fore daylight and in de fields til dark.

I heard my mudder say dat the mistress was a fine woman, but dat de marse was [rigid].

De white folks did not help us to learn to read or write. De furst school I remember dat wuz accessbile was foh 90 days duration. I could only go when it wuz too wet to work in de fields. I wuz bout 16 years when I went to de school.

Der wuz no church on de plantation. Couldn't none of us read. But after de surrender I remember de furst preacher I ebber heard. I remember de text. His name was Charles Fletcher. De text was "Awake thou dat sleepeth, arise from de dead and Christ will give you life!" ...

After de surrender my mother tole me dat the marse told de slaves dat dey could buy de place or dey could share de crops wid him and he would rent dem de land....

Abraham Lincoln fixed it so de slaves could be free. He struck off de handcuffs and de ankle cuffs from de slaves. But how could I be free if I had to go back to my massa and beg for bread, clothes and shelter? It is up to everybody to work for freedom.

I think it's a good thing dat slavery is ended, for God hadn't intended there to be no man a slave.[6]

Perry Sid Jemison's words give a glimpse into what life was like for our own ancestors during slavery. Food was often scarce, illiteracy was the standard, and whether or not religion was taught depended on the slave owner. Slavery afforded very few choices for people about their own lives; they were regarded as the property of someone else.

Life was not easy for our ancestors during slavery or during the reconstructive period afterward. They worked so hard and much of the time got so very little, if anything, in return. Yet they pressed on with hope for something better all the time, and that hope translated into extraordinary action in Sherman and Callie Booker's case. With faith in the Lord and a great deal of sacrifice, they freed themselves and their family from a plight that many people still face today: the destructive grasp of debt. I am so grateful for them and all that they did to show us that freedom from any heavy burden is possible. ✽

DANIEL BOOKER

You have seen how a man was made a slave; you shall see how a slave was made a man.
–Frederick Douglass –

ALTHOUTH the Atlantic Slave Trade was legally outlawed in America on January 1, 1808, the trading of slaves within the United States grew and prospered. The "Middle Passage" across the Atlantic Ocean from Africa to the Americas was horrifying, with many people being stolen from their homes, separated from their families, sold to European traders, and exported thousands of miles on ships in inhumane conditions to become property. Virginia relied heavily on slave labor to produce crops, which is where Daniel Booker was born in 1819.

Daniel was born a slave in a state that was known for its plantations and importation of slaves. Virginia had become one of the largest producers and exporters of tobacco in the United States, and by the 1800s was facing an overabundance of the crop—and of its slave labor force—resulting in economic losses. Many farmers decided to move southwest into southern Georgia and central Alabama to expand their plantations and grow different crops. These areas were already occupied with Native Americans, largely of the Creek Nation. The farmers who wanted to settle these viewed the Indians as a "problem" and a hindrance to progress, so they pressured the federal government to have them forcefully removed. Andrew Jackson, who would later become the president of the United States, led a portion of the U.S. military forces to battle the Creeks for their land. The Creeks lost 22 million acres of land in their defeat. They hoped that by signing a treaty to give up this land, they would be able to retain other lands and avoid further harassment.[1] From 1817, when the treaty was signed, until well into the 1840s, people bought this land in Alabama, hoping to start a new prosperous life for themselves in agriculture.

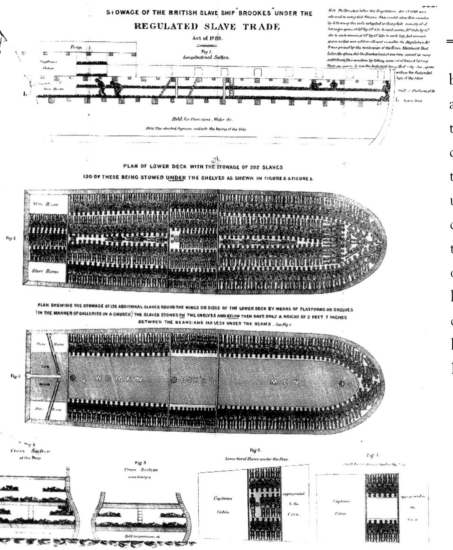

STOWAGE OF THE BRITISH SLAVE SHIP "BROOKES" UNDER THE
REGULATED SLAVE TRADE
Act of 1788.

This migration of farmers led to a booming domestic slave trade, known as the "Second Middle Passage." Slave traders sold slaves from the Atlantic coastal states to plantation owners in the Deep South, once again breaking up families and forcing slaves to undergo horrendous conditions while travelling on foot to work for a new owner. Virginia became one of the largest exporters of slaves, and it was during this time that Daniel was sold, likely by an owner whose surname was Booker (as there were many slavehold-

A sketch of a British slave ship. This ship was designed to transport a total of 422 slaves. They were crammed into disgusting, inhumane living conditions for three to six months; many men and women died during the voyage. Slaves who arrived from the 'old country' were referred to by American-born slaves as 'saltwater niggers.'
(Courtesy Library of Congress)

ing Bookers in Virginia in the 1820s), to a new owner in Alabama.

Reverend Oliver Welch was one of the farmers who, along with his family, made the move from Virginia to Alabama in the early 1830s. This move turned out to be a profitable decision for the Welch family: Oliver and his sons ended up becoming some of the largest slave holders in Talladega County. In 1840 Oliver owned 49 slaves; by 1860 he and his three sons who lived nearby—Nathaniel, William A., and James E.—had a total of 118 slaves. Each of these men possessed a value of his combined real estate and personal property over $40,000. That would be the equivalent of an estate worth over $1 million in 2009.[2] This fortune was built upon the backs of the human beings he treated as property, like Daniel, who was likely sold to this family in the early 1830s.

Family and children seemed to be a very important part of Daniel's life, even in the midst of the uncertainty of slavery. Having been sold once before, perhaps he took this to heart and did his best to keep his family together. Daniel's first "wife" (marriages of slaves were not legally recognized) was a woman born in Virginia whose name is unknown because she likely died before her name could be listed on a census. She was the mother of his first three children: John, Dave, and Julia Ann. As recorded on the 1870 census, Dave

Daniel Booker picked cotton in Alabama in a field like this one.

and John Booker and their young families were living on either side of Daniel Booker's family. It was common at that time for children to continue to live near their families for several years, to farm with them, and to share the use of farm equipment. This is evident on several mortgage records in Talladega County on which Daniel Booker is listed with one or two of his sons. Daniel's daughter, Julia Ann Booker, also lived near him in the 1866 and 1870 censuses with her husband, Phillip Long.[3]

Sometime shortly after his first wife died, Daniel married Rachael Welch. There was a significant difference in their ages—Daniel was 33, and Rachael was 17—but this was a common pattern when a husband was widowed and had small children. Together they had nine children: Thomas, Basil M., Lafayette, Robert Lee, William Sherman, Wesley Scott, Frank, Nannie, and Ann E. Booker. Four of their children were born before the end of slavery.

Before slavery ended in 1865, Daniel and

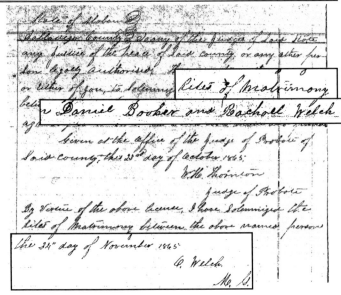

Daniel Booker and Rachael Welch were legally married on November 24, 1865 by Oliver Welch.
(Courtesy of Talladega County Clerk of Probate Court)

Rachael were considered property, so tracing their history is a challenging task. They were legally married on 24 November 1865, and from their marriage record we learn that they were married by "Rev. O. Welch." Oliver Welch was not only one of the larg-

Slave children pose behind large kettles used for boiling laundry on the plantation.

est slaveholders in Talladega county, he was also the minister of the Alpine Baptist Church. Given that Rachael shares his surname, we can assume that she was owned by him or one of his sons, and that it was likely that Daniel Booker and his children born in slavery were also owned by the Welch family. Looking at the 1850 census, it is evident that Dr. William A. Welch, one of Rev. Oliver Welch's sons, owned

slaves that almost exactly matched the ages of Daniel, Rachel, John, Dave, Julia Ann, and is confirmed on the 1860 census with the addition of Thomas and Basil M.

In addition, church records exist from baptisms and other events that took place at the Alpine Baptist Church, where Oliver Welch was the pastor and his son, William, was a deacon. This gives us additional clues into the lives of our ancestors:

> Those baptized on October 13 were Catherine Mallory, John H. Watkins, William Derrick, and Adaline Derrick. One day earlier, Thomas H. Reynolds and Morgan Reynolds were baptized. Blacks who were received into the fellowship of the church were Ellick, Austin, and Peggy, who belonged to Cunningham Wilson; Daniel, who belonged to Dr. William A. Welch.[4]

This highly suggests that Daniel Booker was owned by William Welch. Phillip Long (Daniel's son-in-law), his brother Tipton Long, and Tipton's wife, Arabella Welch, were also owned by William Welch,[5] further confirming the ties between these

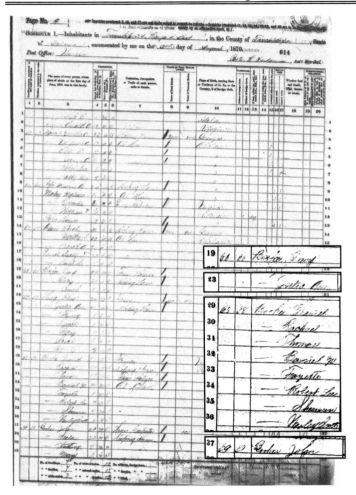

families.

Though we don't know very much about their owner, Dr. William A. Welch, we know that he was described by his family as "a country doctor loved and honored by all who knew him."[6] He was also someone with which the Booker family stayed in relatively close contact after slavery. In 1872, Charlotte Booker was married to Jeff Dudley by Rev. Oliver Welch at the home of Dr. William A. Welch. In many marriage records of African-Americans in Talladega County after slavery, former slaves who had at least amicable connections with their former masters were married at their homes. With all of this information, it becomes practically undeniable that William A. Welch owned this family.

Despite the seemingly positive relationships that some African-Americans had with their former masters after emancipation, slavery was still a horrendous

1870 US census record in Alabama listing Daniel Booker and all of his children. (Courtesy of Ancestry.com)

institution that devalued individuals and inflicted deep wounds not only on our ancestors, but on our entire country.[7] I like to think that the following experience, which is a true account taken from the journal of Oliver Welch, was a way of giving back a little bit of the justice deserved by the men who owned and mistreated our ancestors:

About 5 o'clock on Thursday evening while Reverend Oliver Welch, Nathaniel Welch [his son], Col Christie and Mrs. D. Gorman were sitting in the room of the Depot at Alpine[,] a bolt of lightning struck the stove pipe and came down into the room

Dr. William A. Welch

with terrible violence— Rev. Mr. Welch who was sitting with his hands crossed upon his abdomen was stricken on the left arm just below the joint— the fluid tearing off the skin and bruising the flesh down to the hand. One finger was cut nearly off and both hands injured and cut in many places. The abdomen where his hands rested is severely bruised. The current then passed through the floor immediately under Mr. Welch's foot making a hole in the plank some fifteen inches long and an inch or an inch and a half wide.

Mr. Nat Welch, who was standing near was stricken on the hip, the current burning a furrow down in the heel, a part of which was cut out. The clothes of those persons were torn to shreds. The sleeves [were] reduced to fragments. The spectacle's case in Mr. O. Welch's pocket flattened and melted at both sides.

The other persons present were stunned and shocked but sustained no permanent injury. . . Mr. Nat Welch is doing well but his father's injuries being so extensive and numerous, his condition is somewhat critical. His numerous friends sympathize with him and hope he and his son may soon be well.[8]

Once slavery ended, former slaves like Daniel

Rev. Oliver Welch

had to make a living for themselves, and many times the only option available was sharecropping. Daniel rented a plot of land on which he would raise crops, and in turn he had to pay for the use of the land with some amount of the cotton that he raised. Daniel frequently had to mortgage his property—borrowing the money to pay for renting the land against the cotton that he would potentially grow in the coming season as collateral. In addition, Daniel sometimes had to buy seed, farming equipment, and clothing from the plantation store on credit, further adding to his expenses. At the end of the harvesting season, the landowners weighed the crop and determined how much they were worth; they also kept the financial records. When debts were to be paid, few tenant farmers broke even. Daniel was forced to mortgage still more of his possessions: the cotton crop and the corn crop, along with his mule. Each season, tenant farmers went further into debt as they gave what

little they made to the landowners as payment for use of their land, and their debts became yet another form of bondage.

Still, this life was better than a life of slavery, because at least Daniel's family was his own, not the property of his slave master. Daniel and Rachael had

White landowner weighing sharecroppers' cotton. Landowners frequently kept sharecroppers in debt on purpose.

the opportunity to teach their children to value their relationship with God, and as a result two of their sons were greatly involved in church matters. John Booker, Daniel's oldest son, purchased a church building and surrounding land in Talladega County. Later on, Basil M. Booker felt called to the ministry and served as the second pastor of the Mount Olive Baptist Church in Sycamore, Alabama. The Booker family attended this congregation for generations. It still stands today as a testimony of the faith of our forebears, as well as a reminder to continue to teach our own families to grow in our love for God, to rejoice in gospel of Jesus Christ, and to be engaged in serving others.

Even though he grew up in slavery and then lived most of his live as a sharecropper, Daniel Booker still left behind a legacy of hard work, as well as the importance of building a relationship with God. Almost all of Daniel's sons were able to escape from the sharecropping system to become landowners at some point in their lives. That is no small accomplishment when you've had seven sons!

As I have learned about Daniel and Rachael Booker, I have felt love for them and a sense of pride in who they were. I feel their strength encouraging us to not let our heads hang down in discouragement when setbacks come, but to keep moving forward to see the day when our children can have a better life than we have. They would want us to teach our children truth and good principles by which they can guide their lives through difficult times, as they taught their children, and through which their children were able to prosper and provide for their posterity. I look forward to the day when I will meet them and learn firsthand of their experiences, trials, and triumphs here on earth.❄

SECTION THREE:

JOSIE ESTELL

The highest and noblest work in this life is that of a mother
–Russell M. Nelson –

JOSIE Estell's life can be summed up in one word: *family*. Born in 1894[1] in Wewoka, Alabama, Josie grew up with her parents, Es and Fannie, who did their best to nurture her and teach her to love and respect them and her siblings. She was the fourth of seven children, and the family was very closely knit. Even after she and her brothers and sisters married and had their own children, several of them lived very close to one another, so their children were also close.

Josie had a strong appreciation for family and its importance, so it is not surprising that she married early. In 1908, she caught the eye of a young man named Joseph Booker who lived nearby in Sycamore. Even though Josie was still very young, she was beautiful. She had a friendly personality, in addition to her lovely brown skin and long, dark hair.[2] She had already learned from her mother how to keep up a household, so by the standards of the day, she was ready to become a wife. Josie and Joe Booker were married in November of 1908 in Sycamore by Joe's uncle, Basil M. Booker, who was the pastor of the Mount Olive Baptist Church.

Josie was only about 15 years old at the time of her marriage, and Joe was 21. Exactly one year later, they welcomed their first child, Margie Estella Booker, into their family. This was just the beginning of Josie's calling to bring children into the world and raise them with love, a cause for which she would literally give her life.

Margaret Willis Collection

Charlenia Demps was often told that she looked like her grandmother, Josie Estell.

Just after Christmas in 1910, when Josie was about seven months pregnant with her second child, Frank, Margie fell sick with pneumonia. There were few medical treatments at this time, especially for people living in rural communities. Antibiotics did not yet exist, so they might have wrapped her in a blanket and sat with her in the sun during the day, encouraging her to cough.[3] Her condition worsened, though, and all they could do was comfort her as her little body coughed for days. On January 4th, 1911, Margie Estella Booker died at fourteen months old. Josie must have felt consuming pain in losing

"Indian in the Family"

Many people have attributed Josie Estell's long, straight hair to having "Indian in the family." In fact, that is a common statement I have heard among African-Americans when explaining straight hair, lighter skin tone, or certain facial features that would not be classified as characteristically "African." It is true that in the past there was some mixing between slaves of African descent and Native Americans, but most of that occurred in the late 1700s and early 1800s, and would not have much affect on the physical appearance of a descendent living 150 years later. In truth, much of what is attributed to mixing with Native Americans is really the result of mixing caused by white slave owners. Es Estell, his siblings, and his mother were all listed as mulatto, or mixed, on census records, and were very light-skinned. Perhaps at some point it became more socially acceptable to be part Indian than to be part white, even though many people were.

This does not mean that none of our ancestors were Native American. The land that formed Talladega county was taken from the Creek Nation in the early 1800s and sold off in pieces to people moving west, hoping to cash in on the rich soil by growing cotton. Many of them brought slaves with them, like John Estill and Daniel Booker. It is possible that some of the Native Americans stayed behind and formed relationships with slaves brought into the area, and that some of these people could have been our ancestors. So far, the only documentation I have found of any Native American ancestry in the family is a handwritten document from my grandfather, Charles Demps, stating that his grandfather was "3/25 Indian." So until I find further documentation, we will have to live with our ancestors having been mixed. And it is nothing of which we should be ashamed. It is our heritage.

THE STATE OF ALABAMA. TALLADEGA COUNTY.   Marriage License.

To any Licensed Minister of the Gospel in regular Communion with the Christian Church or Society of which he is a member, or Judge of the Supreme, Circuit, or City Court, or Chancellor within the State, or Judge of Probate or Justice of the Peace within their respective Counties—GREETING:

You are hereby authorized to solemnize Marriage between Mr. *Joe Booker* and M. *Josie Estell* and to join them together in Matrimony, and to certify the same in writing to this office, as required by law.

Given under my hand *16* day of *Nov.*, A.D. 19*08*   J. E. CAMP   , Judge of Probate.

This certifies that I have solemnized Marriage between Mr. *Joe Booker* and M. *Josie Estell* according to law, at *Sycamore*, in said County and State, on the *22* day of *Nov.* 19*08*   *B. M. Booker* M. G.

Marriage record of Josie Estell to Joe Booker on 22 Nov. 1908. The marriage was performed by B.M. Booker, Joe's uncle, a pastor at the Mt. Olive Baptist Church in Sycamore, AL. (Courtesy of Talladega County Clerk of Probate Court)

her child, and was surely inconsolable even though she had another child on the way. Yet somehow she pulled herself together, and in March of 1911 she gave birth to Frank.

The addition of children to the family continued every two years like clockwork. Nellie Mae came in May of 1913, and in April of 1915 Joseph followed. A handwritten note by Nellie lists a sister named Ora Mae next, who would have been born in about 1917,[4][5] but she must have also died shortly after birth. In March 1919 came Pearson, Callie in February 1921, and Georgia in January 1923. Richard was born in May 1925, and lastly Fannie in March 1927. She spent twenty years pregnant or nursing her children. And just like most other women of the time, Josie both raised her children and worked hard taking care of her home while her husband worked and took care of the farm. There were no refrigerators or freezers, so she had to cook fresh meals from scratch daily for a family of ten, in addition to doing laundry, cleaning, mending clothes, and taking care of farm animals. Fortu-

Margaret Willis and Rita Morrison Collections

nately, she also had the help of the older children, both with the chores and in taking care of their younger siblings.

The beginning of 1929 was the time when Josie would have been due to have her eleventh child. According to family memory, none of Josie's children really knew what was wrong, but it seems that she was near the end of a pregnancy and complications progressed very quickly. Josie had very likely developed toxemia, a condition otherwise known today during pregnancy as pre-eclampsia. Toxemia is caused by a buildup of toxins in the blood, and this creates a temporary rise in blood pressure during pregnancy. There is also increased fluid retention, and there can be serious damage to various organs in the body as a result of these problems. If it progresses far enough, it puts both the baby and the child at risk of death.[6] The fluid retention caused by toxemia leads to difficulty in the ability to control

Clockwise from top left: Joseph, Pearson, Georgia, Callie, Richard, Nellie, Fannie, Frank.

the bladder and urinate, and this can lead to serious bladder infections.[7]

It is likely that in the weeks before her due date Josie's blood pressure began to rise, and she developed a bladder infection. By the time Josie sought treatment from the doctor, all he could do was test for a bladder infection and drain her bladder. There were no antibiotics for her, and no modern medications to stop the high blood pressure and fluid retention. In modern medicine there are ways to alleviate this problem, such as inducing labor early, but in Josie's case, little could be done.

Several days passed, but Josie's condition only worsened.[8] The symptoms of toxemia usually stop as soon as labor is over, but in Josie's case, it seems the condition had already progressed so far that it was irreversible by the time her body went through this difficult labor. Her blood pressure likely spiked as went into labor with this

Death certificate of Josie Estell Booker. The handwriting is very difficult to decipher, but it is clear that she died from some sort of bladder problem that lasted only a week, and it seems that toxemia contributed to her death. She was buried in the Wilson Cemetery.
(Courtesy of Alabama Center for Health Statistics)

last child. All Josie's children remember is that there was a lot of blood, but other adults kept them from knowing the full scope of what was happening. The child did not survive. Then, late in the evening of February 15th, 1929, Josie Estell Booker passed away, leaving behind a young husband and eight children, ages one to 17. She was a mother who lived and died for her family.

I have felt a special love and connection to Josie Estell as I have searched out records for her and her family. I feel like I have grown to know her personally as my great-grandmother, and that even though we did not know each other here on earth, I feel that, as one of her descendants and part of her family, I am important to her. I have felt her love, kindness, warmth, and enthusiasm, especially through other members of the Estell(e) family, all of whom seem to share these same traits. She left mortality at a relatively young age, but I look forward to meeting her one day so I can thank her for giving her life to raise children and for being part of the reason why I am in the world today.✿

ES ESTELL & FANNIE PLAYER

Everybody can be great...because anybody can serve. You don't have to have a college degree to serve....You only need a heart full of grace. A soul generated by love.
—Martin Luther King, Jr. —

FROM the first time I heard his name when I was nine years old, I felt a connection to Es Estell. He has been special and important to me, and even though I have never met him, I have always felt a desire to learn about him. It has been a privilege and a blessing to research his life and to talk with people who knew him personally. In some ways, it helps me to feel like I know him now, too.

Contrary to popular belief, Es really did have a name, not just a first initial! He was born Estill Estill in 1861, the second child of John and Matilda Estill, just a few years before the end of slavery. Because his first and last names were the same, he went by "Es" for short. Es was the second of four children and was born into a family

Es made his living as a sharecropper, like his man pictured above.

that very much valued education. By 1870, Es was already in school, reading and writing at the age of nine. This was unusual for black children during this time period and may have been in part because of the family's positive relationship with one of their likely former slave owners, Eudocia Estill.

Es and his younger brother, John Jr., grew up following in the footsteps of their father, both working as farm laborers and struggling to make ends meet in the sharecropping system of rural Alabama. Es also worked in the sawmill on the side. They were very much involved in their church, the Africa Baptist Church. Farm and church work did not get in the way of Es looking for love and companionship, and soon he found himself courting a

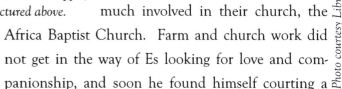

Photo courtesy Library of Congress

young lady named Fannie Player who grew up not too far from his family. She was a hard worker, learning early how to take care of a large family when her mother died fairly young, likely during childbirth. Eventually Fannie's father, Owen, sent all of the children to live with aunts and uncles, and she ended up with her uncle Washington Player. That is where she stayed until she married Es Estell on November 19, 1885.

Es and Fannie built a log home on Ledbetter Road in what used to be known as Wewoka, Alabama (it is now part of Talladega, near Sycamore). They lived very close to Es' family: his

1900 US census record listing Es Estell and his family, as well as his father John, Sr. and brother John, Jr., living nearby with their families. (Courtesy of Ancestry.com)

father lived two doors down on one side, and his brother lived next door on the other side. That gave the ten children Es and Fannie raised—Ada, Henry, Clisbeth ("Clisby"), Josie, Eva, Carson, George, Ulious V. ("U.V." or "Buck"), Sallie June, and Fannie Mae—many cousins to play with as they grew up. Besides raising several children and some of their grandchildren until they were old enough to go to school, they were always involved in their grandchildren's' lives because they all lived so close together.

Es and Fannie's children grew up and started families of their own, but they also lived nearby. Grandkids came to Es and Fannie's home to play on a daily basis. They sometimes rode the horses or spun on the merry-go-round; other times they would play on the see-saw and the rope swing with a wooden seat. Es was skilled in woodworking, so he would cut wood from his land, take it down to the sawmill to cut it, and bring it back up to build with it. Sawmill work is dangerous, and it was during one of these excursions to the sawmill that Es received an injury that he would be known for throughout his life. Es was cutting wood one day when a shard flew up and hit him in the eye, causing him permanent damage. From then on he had to wear an eye patch, and he has been known for having worn the eye patch ever since.

When he wasn't building play structures or toys for his grandchildren, he was delivering food to his children and their families. Es raised cows for both meat and milk, as well as hogs, so when he killed a hog or calf, he shared the meat with all of his family. He also raised corn, watermelon, beans, and other food that Fannie cooked for the family. Fannie knew how to cook good country food like hog tails and cabbage, and while she cooked and worked around the farm she wore "a great big bonnie hat and a bib,"[1] otherwise known as a bonnet and apron. She took the time to teach important homemaking skills to her daughters and granddaughters, particu-

Fannie Player Estell and Es Estell

larly cooking and quilting, and these skills have been passed down through several generations.

Es and Fannie were so committed to taking care of their grandchildren that when their daughter Josie died at the young age of 34, leaving behind 8 children, they moved next door to help take care of them. For 64 years they worked together to raise children and look after the well-being of their family. I believe they have much to show for it. Over fifty years after their passing, their grandchildren still speak of them with love and respect, expressing that they felt cared for by their grandparents. Their grandchildren, great-grandchildren, and continuing descendents are some of the warmest, most caring peo-

---

Es' Other Children

This was a surprisingly difficult topic for me to write about, because it is hard to call into question who someone's parents are and how a person came into existence. Up until a certain point, my research pointed to Es having only seven children. Upon talking to several family members, however, it appears that he had at least ten, in addition to raising his daughter Ada's child, Fannie Mae, who was born out of wedlock.

It is widely known by the Estelle family that George Estelle is Es Estell's son by a woman other than his wife. By 1930, George was married and living with his own wife and children in Risers, Alabama. Also living with them were George's two brothers, Tim and Amos, and a woman named Sallie Pope, listed as George's grandmother. Tim has been confirmed by family members as another of Es's sons, but what is interesting is that in 1920, Amos is listed as Sallie Pope's son. She was also living next door to Es Estell at the time when Tim and George were born. It is possible that George never knew that his 'grandmother' was really his mother.

Another person said to be one of Es' children is Sallie June, who is listed on the 1910 census as "Sallie J. Player" and a cousin to Es and Fannie. This is certainly possible, given that Fannie's maiden name was Player. But if family lore is true and Sallie June really was Es's daughter, Sallie June's mother may have been Fannie's kin.

This pattern of having children out of wedlock or giving an oldest child to one's parents to raise is a repeated pattern in the Estell(e) family across several generations; some of the situations are openly known throughout the family, and some are known to only a few.

ple I have ever met. They take after Es and Fannie's willingness to open up their homes to others and to show love to family, no matter how distant the relationship.

Despite the difficulties that Es and Fannie faced in their own marriage, somehow they were able to commit to caring for their family together until they died. Es passed away in March of 1949; Fannie died just four months later in July. They spent practically their whole lives together, and I believe that they will be blessed in heaven with a posterity who rejoices for their gifts of a lifetime of love, service, and sacrifice.

John Estell, Jr.

The Estell(e) family is enormous, and this history would not be complete without mentioning the contribution that John Estell, Jr. has made to this family. John Jr. was born in October 1867 in Wewoka (near present-day Sycamore) in Talladega county, Alabama. He was close to his brother, Es, as well as to his father, and lived near them for several years while they raised their families.

John Jr. had a sizeable family. He was married three times during his life and had a total of 22 children by them. In 1888 he married Mahala Lawler, the daughter of Alex Lawler, who was the pastor of the Africa Baptist Church. To this marriage eleven children were born: Sadie, Martin, Lawler, Robert, John, William, Lewis, Lutishia, Lezzell, Roosevelt, and Zora Belle. When Mahala passed away, John married Mary Jenkins in 1906, and Mark was born to them. Only a year later John was married to Lubertie Twymon, with whom he lived out the rest of his life. They had ten children together: Clarence, Ora Lucy, Charles S., Lena, Livingston, Odessa, Laura, Dorothy, John Henry, and Edmond.

Sometime between 1920 and 1925, John made the decision to leave behind the farming life and seek better employment opportunities in the North. He moved with his wife and younger children to Detroit, Michigan and settled into a small home on Orleans

Street. John found work as a machinist in a metal factory, which provided enough pay for him to take care of his wife and the five children who were still at home at the time, without any of them having to work.

Even though John Jr. left behind many of his children in Alabama, they remained close enough that his memory stayed alive in the hearts of his grandchildren. On Father's Day in 1971, Lawler Juan Burt, a son of John Estell Jr.'s oldest child Sadie, organized the first Estell(e) family reunion in John's honor. Even then he determined that there were hundreds of people descended from this single ancestor and wanted to begin a tradition of bringing together the members of the family to preserve "a heritage that is great and noble."[2]

July 2008 marked the 37th anniversary of that reunion as the Estell(e) family gathered together in Detroit, Michigan, this time not only to celebrate John Estell, Jr., but to celebrate our common ancestry through his father, John Estill. What a blessing it was to be a part of such a joyous celebration! We truly do have a heritage that is great and noble, and it is a privilege to meet together regularly to keep that heritage alive.

Descendants of John Estell, Jr. (through his son Martin Estell and Martin's daughter, Sadie) at the Estell(e) Family Reunion, July 2008, Detroit, Michigan.

JOHN ESTILL

The power of the ballot we need in sheer defense,
else what shall save us from a second slavery?
–W.E.B. Dubois –

*J*OHN, Charles, and Joseph Estill did every-thing together: they worked together, they lived next door to each other, and they raised their families together. These three brothers were born in Tennessee in 1833, 1834, and 1835, respectively. They were brought to Alabama by their likely owner, Eudocia Estill. Eudocia had made the journey to Alabama with her husband, James, in 1822, but she returned to Tennessee for several years after his passing in 1826. She moved back to Talladega County, Alabama permanently sometime around 1840, where she lived as a widow for the remainder of her life. Although she was a widow, she was not lonely; Eudocia was a devout Methodist, and made her home a "great resort to Christian ministers."[1] She was an avid supporter of the Confederate army during the Civil War, providing meals and clothing to the troops. She also associated with some of the most important political figures of the day: "Presidents Monroe and Jackson were warm personal friends of Mrs. Estill and they had the honor to be entertained by her on more than one occasion."[2] Our ancestors likely associated with two United States presidents, even if it was in the capacity of a servant in bondage.

Sometime after their arrival in Alabama, John, Charles, and Joe Estill were likely sold to Levi W. Lawler, whose family was involved in founding the Alpine Baptist Church. L.W. Lawler served as the

GPB.org and Britannica.com.

Andrew Jackson and James Monroe, the seventh and fifth presidents of the United States, respectively.

clerk of the Church for several years and was chosen on many occasions as a delegate to Baptist conventions. In addition, he served on the Railroad Commission of Alabama, as well as a representative of Talladega in the Alabama House legislature from 1861 to 1865.[3] According to the Church records, slaves named John, Charles, and Joe, all belonging to Levi W. Lawler, were baptized "at the African branch" of the Church in May 1860.[4] [5] This "African branch" was established around 1852 when William Jenkins built a house for the use of black church members who wanted to meet as a separate congregation. The Alpine Baptist Church records that in 1870 this branch became a separate entity completely, and became known as the Africa Baptist Church. John Estill's family attended this church, as well as many of his descendants, and many members of the Estell(e) family still attend this same church today.

John Estill and his brothers still remained close to the Estills who likely brought them to Alabama, even after slavery ended. After the Civil War, John Estill and his family, as well as Charles and Joseph and their families, lived in close proximity with Eudocia Estill and her daughter Caroline Wilson's family. Charles even named one of his daughters Docia,

This photo was taken of the Africa Baptist Church in 1976 to celebrate its 108th anniversary.

Courtesy of The Daily Home

presumably after his former owner. When John's daughter, Laura Estill, married Merchant White in 1875, she was married "at Caroline Wilson's place"[6] in Talladega county. It was not uncommon for freed slaves to be married at the homes of their former owners, even long after slavery had ended.

Some of the most interesting evidence of the close relationship of John Estill and his descendents with the Estills lies on a piece of private land off of Ledbetter Flat Road in Talladega County. Behind a cotton field, on a dirt road and up a hill, lies the Wilson Cemetery, where many of our Estell ancestors are buried. There are both documents and oral histories of grandparents, great-grandparents, cousins, brothers, and sisters being laid to rest there. When driving up to the Wilson Cemetery, on the right-hand side there is a hill, and at the top of the hill rests stone walls enclosing a cemetery. Inside the stone walls there are several tall monuments that have stood preserved over time with the names of

Nathaniel Welch, Cunningham Wilson, and William and Carrie (Estill) Wilson etched into the stone. These were the names of wealthy white landowners and former slave owners from that area of Talladega County.

Across the dirt

Headstone of Nathaniel Welch, former slave owner in Talladega County.

Kristen Andersen collection

road from this cemetery, there is another large hill. My husband, Jon, and I decided to climb the hill to see if we could find the burial grounds of the ancestors for whom I was searching. As we climbed the hill, I saw several medium-sized rocks along the way. I figured they were marking a path up to the top of the hill, where I could suddenly hear the bubbling of a brook. I then knew that this was the location I had heard described as the place where our ancestors were buried. The cemetery was described as being on a large hill, and beyond the hill was the river where baptisms used to take place. But there were no ornate granite monuments and no stone walls. As I looked out over the hill, my eyes were opened to hundreds of slight depressions in the ground, most of which were marked by small rocks like I saw as I climbed up the hill.

Those were the graves of my ancestors. There was no way to distinguish one from another. It was impossible to know where my great grandmother, Josie Estell, or my great-great grandparents, Es and Fannie Estell, were buried. There was nothing to honor their memory but a depression somewhere in the ground and a mossy rock. They were segregated and demeaned even in death, because the color of their skin and the station to which they had been assigned in life. I started to weep.

I had wondered why so many Estells were buried in a cemetery named after a Wilson, a cemetery that was on land once owned by William and Caroline Estill Wilson. Even though the Estills were not the continuous owners of John, Charles, and Joe, they still had a close enough relationship to grant them permission to use the burial grounds set aside for their slaves and the slaves' descendents. I hope to one day place a permanent memorial at the site, so

Kristen Andersen collection

The grave markers of our ancestors—broken rocks with no engraving, covered with decades worth of fallen leaves.

HARPER'S WEEKLY.

JOURNAL OF CIVILIZATION.

Vol. XI.—No. 568.]   NEW YORK, SATURDAY, NOVEMBER 16, 1867.   [SINGLE COPIES TEN CENTS. $4.00 PER YEAR IN ADVANCE.

"THE FIRST VOTE."—Drawn by A. R. Waud.—[See next Page.]

that others will know that our ancestors lived rich and meaningful lives of great worth. They deserve to be remembered.

To relieve my sadness at the separation our ancestors suffered throughout their lives, I turned my thoughts to a hot July day in 1867 when John Estill and his brothers were going somewhere together where they did not need a pass or permission from a master. They no longer had a master! They went together to the county courthouse to register to vote for the first time. The Estill brothers were freed from slavery in 1865 and they were doing their best to prosper and provide for their families during the difficult time of economic and political reform in the South. They each had hope for a better future, and the opportunity to vote was part of having a say in their future.

The United States had granted citizenship to for-

"The First Vote" - *the first election in which freed black men could vote in 1867.* (Courtesy of DailyUSHistory.com)

mer slaves and was making some forward progress by ratifying the 14th and 15th Amendments to the Constitution. African-Americans were supposed to have full protection under the law, and no one was to deny their rights to vote "on account of race, color, or previous condition of servitude."[7] For a short time, while black men were still able to vote, there was some political progress in the South in their behalf. African-Americans were the majority in several southern states; as a result, in 1870 several black men were elected to serve in the U.S. House of Representatives, and a black senator was elected in Mississippi.[8]

John Estill and his brothers, Charles and Joseph, registered to vote together on July 25, 1867. (Courtesy of the Alabama Department of Archives and History)

Unfortunately, after only a short time, many people sought to take those rights away again, both legally and illegally. Starting in 1870, states began to pass amendments to their constitutions in an effort to disenfranchise African-Americans. It became not only difficult for blacks to vote, but life-threatening. There was incessant racism in the South, and in or-

der to keep blacks from mobilizing for change, whites instituted certain requirements that many blacks could not meet. Because many black Americans in the late 1800s and early 1900s were poor sharecroppers, they created poll taxes, which prohibited anyone from voting unless they could pay the determined fee. This worked unfavorably against poor white voters as well. There were oral literacy tests

White citizen league barring black voters. From Harper's weekly, October 1874. Note sign on door: "Notice No Nigger Voters Allowed Here."

that were nearly impossible to pass because they were often made purposely unfair. The Grandfather Clause was also instituted, requiring that unless your ancestors were able to vote before 1867 (which was the year that the first freed slaves were allowed to register to vote in Alabama), men seeking to vote had to take the literacy tests and meet certain property requirements in order to vote. All of this was in addition to the outright threats of violence that discouraged most black men from voting, as sometimes election officials would publish African-Americans' names in local newspapers, and their intention to vote would be brought to the attention of the Ku Klux Klan.[9]

By 1910, Alabama, Mississippi, North and South Carolina, Virginia, Louisiana, Georgia, and Oklahoma had all passed laws successfully circumventing the nation's constitution and barring blacks and other minorities from voting.[10] But the legacy still remains that our ancestors were brave enough to take that opportunity while they had it.

John Estill took part in this important part of history, valuing the right to vote and to use his voice and power to effect change in whatever ways he could. When I found his name alongside his brothers' names on the voter registration papers, I felt inspired. I don't want to take for granted the freedom that I have today to walk into my local polling place and vote. This right, which we cast aside as unimportant or talk ourselves into believing won't make a difference, was so powerful in the hands of our ancestors that states had to pass laws and use violence to stop them. We can make our voices heard, just like our forefathers did, and make a lasting positive impact for the generations who follow us. ❧

AFTERWORD

If we have the courage and tenacity of our forebears, who stood firmly like a rock against the lash of slavery, we shall find a way to do for our day what they did for theirs.
— Mary McLeod Bethune —

WRITING this book has been the most incredible journey for me, but I have not done it alone. I have had the support of friends and extended family, but I have also felt strength of our ancestors as I have researched their lives. I have felt the desire to walk taller and to find joy in the midst of sorrows as I have uncovered their experiences. They were real people, and even though I did not get to meet many of them in person, the sacrifices that they made in their lives paved the way for me to be who I am today.

I like to think of this picture as a family portrait of all of our ancestors who have passed on. I stumbled upon it one day at an everyday store while taking a break from my research. The landscape pictures a hill, and at the bottom of the hill there is a stream of water where people are being baptized—much like the hill where lies the Wilson Cemetery and the stream where the Estells were baptized. A church stands tall in the background, like the Mount Olive Baptist Church or the Africa Baptist Church, reminding us of their faith. There are even horses grazing in the background, much like the old Jemison farm that was nearby long ago. Their faces are varying shades of brown, just like the faces of our ancestors.

In my mind, these people are raising up their arms in rejoicing because of their joy in accepting baptism, and also in being found by us. Their lives and legacies are no longer forgotten. As I have gotten to know them through records and stories, again I feel the truth of the words of the prophet Malachi

Photo opposite page: Unknown artist

in the Bible: "Behold, I will send you Elijah the prophet before the coming of...the Lord: And he shall turn the heart of the fathers to the children, and the heart of the children to their fathers" (Malachi 4:6).

I know that as we research our ancestors, our hearts are turned to them and we get to know and love them as if we had known them during this life. In turn, their hearts are turned to us, and we can feel their support, strength and wisdom in our daily lives. We will see them again after this life. They will know us, and we can know them and thank them for their contributions to our lives. Let us lift up our hands and rejoice with them. ✝

NOTES

Charles William Demps

1. The Sylacauga Chamber of Commerce, "The Marble Industry in Sylacauga: A Story of Its Growth, People and Contributions," *Sylacauga.net*, http://www.sylacauga.net/chamber/marble_industry.htm (accessed 6 February 2008).

2. J. Leigh Mathis-Downs, *Childersburg* (Charleston, SC: Arcadia Publishing, 2006), 9, http://books.google.com/books?id=...r4QFICYbewOtEcKCbRsjd HWXIY4 (accessed 8 January 2008).

3. Stephen Meyer, "The Degradation of Work Revisited: Workers and Technology in the American Auto Industry, 1900-2000," http://www.autolife.umd.umich.edu/Labor/L_Overview/L_Overview8.htm (accessed 26 March 2009).

Henry Lewis Demps, Jr. and Annie Belle Magruder

1. "Alabama Moments in American History," 2001, *Alabama Department of Archives and History*, http://www.alabamamoments.alabama.gov/sec69nt.html (accessed 5 April 2008).

2. "Who Were The Tuskegee Airmen?," *Tuskegee Airmen Website*, http://www.tuskegeeairmen.orgTuskegee_Airmen_History .html (accessed 7 April 2008).

Henry's Brothers: James, Benjamin, Lem, & Ludie Demps

1. Philip McGuire (ed.), *Taps for a Jim Crow Army: Letters from Black Soldiers in World War II* (University Press of Kentucky, 1993), 146.

2. Tracy Kidder, "Soldiers of Misfortune," *The Atlantic* (March 1978) , p. 3, http://www.theatlantic.com/doc/197803/tracy-kidder-soldiers/3 (accessed 4 February 2009).

3. "STD Facts: Syphilis," *Centers for Disease Control*, http://www.cdc.gov/std/syphilis/STDFact-Syphilis.htm (accessed 5 February 2009).

4. "Research Ethics: The Tuskegee Syphilis Study," *Tuskegee University*, http://www.tuskegee.edu/global/story.asp?s=1207598 (accessed 5 July 2010).

5. Stephen B. Thomas, "Anatomy of an Apology: Reflections on the 1997 presidential apology for the syphilis study at Tuskegee" (1999), 1, *Emory University*, http://www.emory.edu/ACAD_EXCHANGE/1999/sept99/anatomy.html (accessed 11 February 2008).

6. "The Second Great Migration," *In Motion: The African American Migration Experience*, http://www.inmotionaame.org/migrations/topic.cfm?migration=9&topic=5&tab=image (accessed 1 April 2008).

7. "Mount Vernon Arsenal-Searcy Hospital Complex," *Wikipedia.org*, http://en. wikipedia.org/wiki/Mount_Vernon _Arsenal-Searcy_Hospital_Complex (accessed 20 March 2008).

8. See article, Maisel, Albert Q, "Bedlam 1946," *LIFE Magazine* (6 May 1946), p. 102, *Google Books*, http://books.google.com/books?id=BlUEAAAAMBAJ&printsec=frontcover#v=onepage&q&f=false (accessed 5 July 2010).

9. Leupo, Kimberly, "The History of Mental Illness," *Kathi's Mental Health Review website*, http://www.toddlertime.com/advocacy/hospitals/Asylum/history-asylum.htm (accessed 5 July 2010).

Henry Demps

1. Booker T. Washington, *The Booker T. Washington Papers: 1889-1895*, ed. Louis R. Harlan and Raymond W. Smock, (University of Illinois Press, 1974), 558-559.

2. "Famous Prince Hall Affiliated Free Masons," *Most Worshipful Prince Hall Grand Lodge of Ohio webpage*, http://www.phaohio. org/mwphgloh/likfm.html (accessed 1 March 2008).

3. "Prince Hall Masonic Statistics," *Paul M. Bessel's Homepage*, http://bessel.org/phastats.htm (accessed 1 March 2008).

John Demps

1. Ira Berlin, *Slaves Without Masters: The Free Negro in the Antebellum South* (New York: Pantheon Books, 1974).

2. See article, "After 40 years, interracial marriage flourishing," *MSNBC.com* (15 April 2007), http://www.msnbc.msn. com/id/18090277/ (accessed 26 March 2009). The ban on interracial marriage in Virginia was overturned by the Supreme Court in 1967. It was not lifted in South Carolina until 2000 and in Alabama until 2001, with 40% of Alabama's population objecting to lifting the ban.

3. Marina Wikramanayke, *A World in Shadow: The Free Black in Antebellum South Carolina* (Columbia, S.C.: University of South Carolina Press, 1973), 13-14.

4. "University of South Carolina Archaeologists Locate Confederate Cannons, Naval Yard," 5 June 2009, *Midlandsbiz*, http://www.midlandsbiz.com/news/headlines/375/ (accessed 5 July 2010).

Nellie Mae Booker

1. On the 1930 U.S. Census, Nellie's occupation is listed as "home keeper."

2. Nellie Mae Booker Demps, in discussion with author, 23 May 2003.

Joe Booker

1. Booker T. Booker Jr., in telephone discussion with the author, December 21, 2007.

2. Emily Oswalt, "Northeast Alabama Cotton Mills," *Personal Home Page*, http://www.geocities.com/emily_oswalt/index. html (accessed 13 June 2008).

3. These occupations are listed in the 1930 census in Manhattan, NY on the pages including Thomas and Willie Booker.

William Sherman Booker

1. Quote from Talladega County Mortgages, Book 6, p. 599-600.

2. Booker T. Booker, Jr., phone discussion.

3. Henry Louis Gates, *African American Lives*, DVD, Directed by Jesse Sweet, Leslie D. Farrell, Leslie Asako Gladsjo, and Graham Judd (PBS Home Video; Paramount Home Entertainment, 2006).

4. See "Helen Jemison Meier Family Tree: Robert Jemison 1749-1799," *Ancestry.com*, http://trees.ancestry.com/pt/person. aspx?tid=4440555&pid=-1603268251 (accessed 12 February 2008). Samuel Jemison, owner of Perry Sid Jemison, died in Perry county, Alabama on 18 September 1855. His nephew, Shadrack Mims Jemison, died in Talladega county, Alabama on 23 October 1897.

5. "African American Lives."

6. "Jemison, Sid Perry," *Access Genealogy: Ohio Slave Narratives*, 2007, http://www.accessgenealogy.com/scripts/data/database. cgi?file=Data&report=SingleArticle&ArticleID=0028208 (accessed 12 February 2008).

Daniel Booker

1. "People & Events: Indian removal 1814 – 1858," *Africans In America Home Page*, http://www.pbs.org/wgbh/aia/part4/4p2959.html (accessed 26 May 2008).

2. Samuel H. Williamson, "Six Ways to Compute the Relative Value of a U.S. Dollar Amount, 1774 to present," *Measuring Worth*, 2008, http://www.measuringworth.com/uscompare/ (accessed 26 March 2009).

3. John and David Booker have been linked to the family through census records, as well as a mortgage record in which together they borrow $250 "for the purpose of making a crop this year." Julia Ann appears in several public family trees on Ancestry.com. Given the close proximity in which she lived to Daniel Booker and her listing in these family trees, I have assumed that she was his daughter.

4. James Mallory, Grady McWhiney, Warner O. Moore, and Robert F. Pace, *Fear God and Walk Humbly: The Agricultural Journal of James Mallory, 1843-1877* (Tuscaloosa, AL: University of Alabama Press, 1997), 539, ttp://www.netlibrary.com (accessed 26 March 2008).

5. Mallory, 596.

6. "Dr. William A. Welch," *FindAGrave.com*, http://www.findagrave.com/cgi-bin...n&GRid=8539227& (accessed 20 March 2008).

7. See Wendell Berry, *The Hidden Wound* (New York: North Point Press, April 1, 1989). An excellent book on this subject.

8. Qtd. in Mallory, 600-601.

Josie Estell

1. Josie was born in 1894 according to the 1900 census.

2. Louise White, in discussion with Jonathan Andersen, July 24, 2008.

3. According to Ignazio Rallo, who contracted pneumonia as a child in the 1920s, antibiotics were unavailable for

treating pneumonia, so his mother would take him out in the sun for several hours each day, encouraging him to cough. Ignazio made it through the disease; unfortunately, Margie Estella didn't.

4. According to handwritten notes of Nellie Booker Demps, Josie had a daughter named Ora Mae between Joseph and Pearson, which is supported by differences in Joseph and Pearson's ages. I have not yet located a death record for Ora.

5. Joe Booker's 1917 World War I draft registration lists that he is supporting a "wife and 4 children." By 1917, Margie Estella had already died, so the only four children could have been Frank, Nellie, Joseph, and Ora Mae.

6. "Gestational Diabetes: Glossary of Terms," *The Plus Size Pregnancy Web Site*, June 2007, http://www.plus-size-pregnancy. org/gd/gdglossary.htm (accessed 26 March 2008).

7. "(Severe?) Toxemia after delivery," *OBGYN.net*, 06 Sep 2001, http://forums.obgyn.net/pregnancy-birth/P-B.0109/0585. html (accessed 26 March 2008).

8. Hollick, Frederick. *The Origin of Life and Process of Reproduction in Plants and Animals...and Cure of the Special Diseases to which It Is Liable* (Philadelphia: David McKay, 1878 or 1902), page 826, http://books.google.com/books?id=...M1 (accessed 26 March 2008). This section mentions the effects of bladder problems and their ability to cause death.

Es Estell

1. Louise White, in discussion with Jonathan Andersen, July 24, 2008.

2. From the typed program of the first Estell Family reunion in 1971.

John Estill

1. Obituary, "Franklin County TN Archives Obituaries: Estill, Eudocia 'Docia' [Mrs. James] August 17, 1886," *The US Gen Web Archives Project*, http://files.usgwarchives.net/tn/franklin/obits/e/estill356gob.txt (accessed 26 March 2009).

2. Obituary, "Estill, Eudocia 'Docia' [Mrs. James]."

3. Thomas McAdory Owen and Marie Bankhead Owen, *History of Alabama and dictionary of Alabama biography, Volume 2*, (Chicago: S. J Clarke Publishing Company, 1921), pages 1157 and 1295, http://books.google.com/books?

id=NloTAAAAYAA....levi%20w.%20lawler&f=false (accessed 9 July 2010).

4. Casey W. Arnette, *The Tie that Binds: History of the Alpine Baptist Church 1832-1988*, 90-91.

5. Another interesting baptism to note is that of L.W. Lawler's Mahala in 1845 (Arnette, 54). Mahala is repeatedly used to name women in the Estell family.

6. From marriage record of Charlotte Booker and Jeff Dudley, 3 August 1872, Talladega County Marriage Records, volume D, page 182.

7. "U.S. Constitution—Amendment 15," *U.S. Constitution Online*, http://www.usconstitution.net/xconst_Am15.html (accessed 27 July 2010).

8. "African Americans in the United States Congress," *Wikipedia.org*, http://en.wikipedia.org/wiki/African_Americans_in _the_United_States_Congress (accessed 27 March 2009).

9. 5. Micheal Jay Friedman, "The Voting Rights Act in Perspective" (June 7, 2007), *The International Information Programs Page*, http://usinfo.state.gov/scv/Archive/2005/Aug/15-884794.html (accessed 20 March 2008).

10. "Disenfranchisement of African American Voters in the Reconstructed South," *Just The Beginning Foundation*, http://www. jtbf.org/index.phpsubmenu=Slavery...=Exhibit (accessed 27 March 2009).

ADDITIONAL RESOURCES

Ancestry.com

Banks, Doris. Interview by author. Detroit, MI, October 2007 and July 2008.

Booker, Richard, Telephone interview by author, March 2008.

Center for Southern African American Music Video Collection. *University of South Carolina.* http://www.sc.edu/csam/archive_video.html (accessed 5 April 2008).

Curry, Charlenia. Interview by author. Southfield, MI, March 2008.

Demps, Nellie Booker. Interview by author. Detroit, MI, May 2003 and Livonia, MI, February 2007.

Estelle, U.V. Jr. Interview by author. Talladega, AL, 22 December 2007

Footnote.com

Gudiel-Teo, Lena. Interview by author. Talladega, AL, 21 December 2007.

HeritageQuest.com

Lyles, Patricia. Telephone interview by author. February 2008.

"The Lynching Century: African Americans Who Died in Racial Violence in the United States, 1865-1965." *African Americans Lynched 1865-1965.* http://www.geocities.com/Colosseum/Base/8507/NLists.htm (accessed 26 March 2009).

Morrison, Lynette. Interview by author. Chicago, IL, March 2008.

Peterson, Mary J. Interview by author. Chicago, IL, March 2008.

Pilot.familysearch.org

Taylor, Quintard. "African American History Timelines." *BlackPast.org.* http://www.blackpast.org/?q=african-american-history-timeline-home-page (accessed 2 January 2008).

Towns, Carol. Telephone interview by author. January 2008.

"Tuskegee Study of Untreated Syphilis in the Negro Male." <u>*Wikipedia.org*</u>. http://en.wikipedia.org/wiki/Tuskegee_Study_of_Untreated_Syphilis_in_the_Negro_Male (accessed 11 February 2008).

"Union Regimental Histories: The United States Colored Troops Infantry." *The Civil War Archive Home Page*. http://www.civilwararchive.com/Unreghst/uncolinf4.htm (accessed 26 May 2008).

Willis, Margaret. Interview by author. Detroit, MI, September 2007 and 22 December 2007

White, Louise. Interview by Jonathan Andersen. Detroit, MI, 26 July 2008.

WorldVitalRecords.com

"World War II Industrial Facilities: Authorized Federal Funding." 21 February 2007. *Heritage Research Center Ltd.* http://www.heritageresearch.com/War%20Facilities.html (accessed 6 February 2008).

Multimedia

Gandy Dancers. Online streamed film. Produced by Barry Dornfield and Maggie Holzberg-Call (1994; New York, NY: Cinema Guild, Inc, 1994). *Folkstreams.net*. http://www.folkstreams.net/film,101 (accessed 27 July 2010).

Gates, Jr., Henry Louis. *African American Lives 2*. DVD. Directed by Graham Judd, Jack Youngelson, Jesse Sweet, Leslie Asako Gladsjo (Hollywood, CA: Paramount Home Entertainment, 2008).

Miss Evers' Boys. DVD. Directed by Joseph Sargent (1997; New York, NY: HBO Home Video, 2002).

Tuskegee Airmen. DVD. Directed by Robert Markowitz (1995; New York, NY: HBO Home Video, 2001).

ALPHABETICAL INDEX

Italics denote photo or record

Made in the USA
Charleston, SC
23 September 2010